# DRAGON SLAYER

## *WARRIOR FOR THE LORD*

## VOLUME II – THE 8TH GATE OF HELL

## LYSSA-ANN CLARKE

ISBN 978-976-96216-8-8 (Paperback)

ISBN 978-976-96216-9-5 (EBook

*This book is dedicated to the Slaves who disappeared from the *Paradise plantation in Jamaica in the 1800's in particular the unaccounted slaves between 1831-1832[1]*

---

[1] Fictitious name used for confidentiality reasons

# Table of Contents

Acknowledgements


*Thanks to the Mission Team, the Generals who mentored me during the 8th Gate missions, my editor and motivator, Jesus my King and the Holy Spirit the great teacher in my life.*

*The completion of this book would not have happened in May 2020 without you playing the integral role you had in providing the experiences for the material and in encouraging me to press on despite the challenges faced in the production of this series*

# CHAPTER 1 -INTRODUCTION

On a tiny island situated within the Caribbean Sea stood a beautiful city that was itself an island of sorts as it was surrounded by water and full of lush hills, greenery and tropical flowers of all sorts and fragrances.

Like the rest of the island, the city of Paradise was filled with migrants and descendants from the continent of Africa who came to the island on huge slave ships through a route known as the middle passage. Most of the slaves came from the West Coast of Africa and were from various tribes. Some were aggressive others were not.

The many men women and children traversed the stormy seas lying down in cramped quarters.

They came to work on the Sugar and Coffee plantations that were owned by British and Scottish nationals who were considered investors in the island which was a British Colony.

The slaves were dispersed throughout the island to work cultivating sugar, coffee, indigo and food provisions. There they worked under extremely harsh conditions and treatment. All were expected to work even the children. Refusal to work could result in the loss of one's life or severe punishment including the treadmill, being whipped or even torture. Many slave owners and overseers also raped and bred their female slaves like animals.

The slaves lived in thatched houses. They were considered heathens and barbaric by the colonist, slave hunters and owners who did not respect their culture and way of life that existed in their homeland in Africa.

They had their little plots that they worked near their homes for food and they did not have much social time except on public holidays given by Britain where the slaves got the opportunity to engage in festive displays playing their wooden flutes, banjos, drums and other instruments and doing the Jon dance.

After emancipation the former slaves were taught English which was the native language of their slave owners. Most could not read and practiced their native religious practices which involved worshipping many gods and the use of demonic forces and fallen angels within their religious rites.

The spirits that the Africans engaged caused mysterious deaths and there were many unexplainable happenings including illnesses. Many entered into trances after dancing to the pulsating beat of the drums which spoke to the spiritual realm. Feeding the ancestral spirits rice and rum was commonplace at the very enchanting sessions where the men women children would move with swaying hips and rhythmic feet.

The practice of slavery, oppression and witchcraft in the nation and cities impacted the physical and spiritual environment. This resulted in the economic and spiritual death of the nation and cities. Many families became cursed and were unable to flourish.

In the early days the island had a lot of prosperity. It was rich with wood, water, precious stones, gold, fine food including the best coffee known across the world.

The numerous waterfalls, beaches, mineral springs, forests and scenery made the nation the jewel in the Caribbean. Many visitors came because of its abundance of wealth. Even the Buccaneers who were pirates had their fair share of the jewelled land.

There were a lot of exports to Europe from the little nation which came under attack from time to time by other nations who wanted to make it theirs.

Due to the threat of invasion from other nations who wanted to colonize it through-out the centuries, forts were built by the Europeans all across the island. First, by the Spaniards, then by the British. These forts were not only placed on the coasts as there were known forts placed on hills in rural communities where the Militia Soldiers could see from a far off any ships that may be coming into nation' s waters and prepare and defend the little island through the use of cannons or muskets which the militia soldiers often carried.

**Before the Africans**

The first natives of the jewelled island were Indians. Their population was not large and they were not as strong as the Africans who came to work the fields, hence those who did not escape into the mountains died from overwork, sickness or abuse from the Europeans.

Over the years, the country experienced a lot of disasters. It had hurricanes, earth-quakes, floods, and diseases such as smallpox and cholera which caused a lot of casualties and impacted its growth and development however the things that are seen physically with the naked eye were easily dealt with but this was not so for those happenings which could not be seen with the naked eye as it would take the use of the spiritual eye to see the things in the spiritual invisible realm.

Persons like clergymen, the spiritually gifted, sorcerers, witches, obeah or obimen - the witchdoctor who was considered religious and sometimes the local herbalist, understood that the earth operated on a dual plane.

They understood that there was a force greater than the human being. They knew that the unseen forces that controlled the real world consisted of good and evil, creatures from the dark world and beings from the Kingdom of Light. They saw not only in the spiritual but also the things that happened on planet earth.

Many members of the clergy did not understand the religious rites and practices of the African slaves and witchdoctors. They thought that everything they did was wrong and banned their practices calling it superstitious and having no effect as it is trickery when in fact the real reason Obeys and Myalism were wrong was because the practice evoked demons associated with African gods.

Some of the clergy also practiced evil as they aligned themselves with the god of earthly wealth. They kept secret meetings and did their enchantments in their secret clubs while professing to be Children of Light and even shepherds of the flock. Many were also slave owners thus in many cases playing a dual role of oppressor and shepherd.

What the Europeans also did not understand in regards to alternative healing was that the local herbalists or medicine man received a natural gift from the Source of Light who is everything good and this gift allowed them to learn about the herbs that are used to heal physical diseases. Many herbalists understood that not all illnesses were rooted from a natural cause. This is so because the light within is very important to one's health.

Many of the herbalists who were considered doctors by the slaves were tainted in that they practiced the use witchcraft or magic which involved darkness which tainted the colours of goodness within. The practice engaged the use of the spiritual realm to cause mysterious happenings including the onset of spiritual illnesses and unfortunate situations that could affect several generations of descendants.

The absence of the dominant force of spiritual light at the end of the journey of both the European and African individual impacted his place in the afterlife as there are assigned places for  the spirits of man. Unfortunately, many individuals bond or free on earth who die suddenly, do not immediately go to their assigned location. Some get stuck in between both worlds, both realms because of something called unfinished business. Those persons who are not Children of the Kingdom of Light are considered lost. Unable to find their way to their holding place.

This situation is very distressing because the **men, women and children in this situation receive a lot of torment and are often asked by the leaders in the Kingdom of Darkness to carry out unpleasant and unloving actions,** impacting the natural or physical world and the spiritual world that actually co-exist on the same plane like a world within a world. A world often at war.

### *Genesis 6:5-7*

*5 The LORD saw how great the wickedness of the human race had become on the earth, and that every inclination of the thoughts of the human heart was only evil all the time. 6 The LORD regretted that he had made human beings on the earth, and his heart was deeply troubled. 7 So the LORD said, "I will wipe from the face of the earth the human race I have created – and with them the animals, the birds and the creatures that move along the ground – for I regret that I have made them.*

# CHAPTER 2 – PARADISE ISLE

The Caribbean Island had many rivers, mountains and springs which watered the island. On the eastern part of the island lay a 770 acre property that was owned by a British planter. The planter was very wealthy and had a son who was a top land surveyor in the 1800s.

The planter grew sugarcane, coffee and ground provisions for export. His estate was also well watered and was surrounded by several rivers and trees.

The planter, who was the slave master, lived in a grand Georgian styled house on the top of a hill overlooking the beautiful estate. From the house he could see several mountains and a huge plain that was very gorgeous to look at.

Close to his home the planter had a garden with many tropical flowers and animals such as sheep, goats, and chickens. Nearby he had a road that was used to race horses a river for water and a recreational area

Within another one thousand (1000) metres he built a coffee works where the coffee was processed and a piazza for drying the coffee and cocoa beans used to make exotic beverages. This was close to a very stony river that was filled with precious stones.

Near the river was a burial site which had on it an old well that was used for easy water storage on the plain. After a while, the well was decommissioned because the slave master and overseer would often throw the live slave down the dark well as a form of punishment.

In the 1800's many agents from the Kingdom of light were dispatched to the nation. The agents' mission was to bring the Kingdom of light to the planters and slaves and to promote the introduction of light onto the nation.

Due to this exercise many temples were built. The majority was led by British missionaries. There was however a growing group that was formed by a black American who was formerly a slave who established a kind of independent temple.

An offshoot of an established organization in America however, this was empowered by natives. These individuals realized the benefits to be gained from becoming a part of the Kingdom of Light and their organization started to grow bit by bit across the island but more so in the western part of the island.

Between the period of Christmas of 1831 and January 4, 1832 some local religious leaders of the Kingdom of Light who were slaves decided that they were going to stand up against the institution of slavery which they had heard was abolished by Britain. This led to several plantations and churches being burnt and many slaves were killed on the island.

In terms of casualties a certain number was reported as the crown lost 14 whites while approximately 207 slaves were reported killed and approximately 300 slaves executed. However one is led to question the credibility of the reports as the insurrection as seen as the largest uprising in the Caribbean.

Each year the planters were required to record their stock and crops for the previous March period which was published in a document called an almanac. Other documents were also created by the mother country Britain which gave a history of the colony, the exports, churches, schools and business. Information on disasters were also recorded and the island had a curator who recorded everything including photographs of the Custos and governors, the minerals in the nation, and the surveys done on all parishes and estates.

Between the years 1831-1832 a significant number of slaves went missing on Paradise Isle. They were not recorded either as transferred or sold. In the March 1831 the number of recorded slaves was 167 on Paradise Isle. In 1832 the number fell to 106 with an unusual note that the **_number of enslaved people are unclear._**

The comment above was an interesting note as the difference in the reduction of the slave stock was approximately **61 slaves.** Where could that amount of slaves be held or buried in the beautiful city called Paradise Isle.

No memorial was held for the missing slaves. Their families could not confirm if they ran away or disappeared into thin air. The remaining 106 could only make assumptions as they too were slaves who had no rights.

Could they have known about the inappropriate use of the well on the burial ground and the freshly dug soil on the property that was close to the very stoney river?

In the year 1830 the slave master died in Britain and the property was left in the hands of the executors which included a popular Custos in the nation.

The property was to be given to the slave master's son however this was held up in a court proceeding for a long time because of claims primarily from the slave master's ex-wife, his cousin's husband, his lawyer and the ex-wife's new husband.

This was the start of struggle, stagnation, and uncertainty for the city of Paradise. Imagine a plantation with no official owner at the location during a time of insurrection. The executors of the estate had their own plantations to secure nine (9) and 11 miles away from Paradise Isle.

Imagine one of the largest plantations in the eastern part of the nation without its cruel master during a time of instability.

While nine (9) miles east is a military base; five (5) miles west was a Native Baptist temple and approximately nine (9) miles to the north east a English Baptist temple that lost a member of the temple in the uprising. This was because the Baptists were attributed to starting the insurrection.

It was also stated according to native folklore, that a piece of land near the river was given to a slave by the master. The land was used to erect a Native Baptist temple which was later taken over by an American organization.

British estate records reflect that in 1830 the master's probated will indicated that two of his slaves receive manumission one male and a female.

All the slaves were to go to his sister.

All the paintings were to go to his cousin yet in reality the property transference to the relatives did not happen because the claim on the property held up the process for many years.

In 1837 the parliamentary papers in Britain eventually awarded the estate to four persons; the master's two lawyers, his ex-wife and her new husband.

None of the named awardees received anything the master's son and female cousins died by the time the case was settled and up to 1840 the property was still registered in the slave master's name.

There was stagnation on the land. In the 1930's when the estate was being advertised for sale it was the entire 770 acres being offered. This meant that the estate remained undivided for approximately one hundred years, an entire century!

In 1834 all slaves received emancipation. Slaves were allowed to rent land and plant ground provisions. Temples and schools were built and many slaves learnt to read. This was supposed to be the beginning of prosperity for the nation – or so it seemed.

With the new found freedom came its own set of problems. The funding from the motherland was reduced and whilst the planters were compensated, the slaves who were taken from their homeland and their descendants remained within the country living in poverty.

The Source who is the most powerful being and the creator of the universe, often called Jehovah, sent help to the nation in the form of missionaries to assist in the development of the cities and to relieve the oppression within the communities as there was still a lot of classism and hardship although slavery had officially ended.

Growth was to be had in the community as a school was built on the property given to the manumitted slave. Light in terms of knowledge was on its way for many.

**Guzzum**

Why was there oppression when slavery was abolished? Why did the planters still treat the freedmen harshly and why were the blacks using 'guzzum' power to solve problems physical, emotional economic, social and spiritual in nature.

You may wonder what is guzzum power, if it is real or superstitious in nature. Well, according to folklore on the island guzzum power was obeah or sorcery used by a lot of slaves across the nation and it solved a lot of problems from simple theft through the use of the earth manual and a key to using ancestral familiar spirits to do the necessary.

The practice of the enslaved Africans were handed down throughout the generations.

Items used in the witchcraft rituals included animals such as frogs, lizards, chickens and goats and items such as candles, salt, rings, stones, sulphur, blood, plants, nail, grave dirt, parchment paper a variety of oils including (*Do as I say, Hold Me, Love me oil, Protection oil, Leave Me alone oil, Clearance, Return to me oil*) and the list goes on as the concoctions were numerous, were of different colours, fragrances and some were even mixed with herbal extracts.

Some individuals would go as far as to get special baths from the witchdoctor which was supposed to heal and protect but which caused stagnation and curses on the users and makers as it was not something good and of light.

These practices that impacts the freewill of an individual or causes harm to others are not from the Kingdom of Light and invites evil forces from the Kingdom of darkness onto a location.

Also, engaging in slavery is not of the Kingdom of Light as it is spiritual oppression.

Oppression and the impact of curses have been taught in the earth's operations manual as being something bad however some slave owners justified the act through some statements made in the earth's manual twisted to suit their own agenda.

This nature of the colonists invited the emissaries of the Kingdom of Light to descend on to the nation.

They had one agenda which was to kill steal and destroy. To kill, steal and destroy hope, purpose, families, communities, cities and eventually the entire nation.

The topic of oppression and slavery has been the subject of many individual, historians, groups and societies.

The slave trade has been a long standing business and tradition in many ancient cultures and in modern times although abolished, the practice still occurs and is often a part of a concept considered as human trafficking where the freewill of the worker is lost and the individual often experience some harsh conditions and various forms of abuse.

So it is in the natural, so it is in the physical. If slavery exists in the physical it also exists in the spirit. As a matter of fact it is the things in the spiritual realm that drives the natural realm. However, because the spiritual realm is invisible to the natural eye, the natural man will not be able to see the factors influencing him here on planet earth,

Many of the stories in the earth's manual – particularly the old testament speaks to the oppression of man, God's guidance and provision throughout the period and the deliverance of God's people from the oppressor.

The scriptures are important to learn about methods or strategies of warfare. The lessons learnt from the stories include the fact that God provides, protect, and defends his people who are expected to serve and worship him who need to be obedient, trusting, faithful, loving, truthful and hopeful.

Much could be said about slavery oppression and the afterlife. However, for this book will assess the experience of the missing slaves and how they were released by God.

For more on the topic please see the Visioneers series and for the afterlife the book Paradise at the link below.

**Link to books Amazon:** https://www.amazon.com/s?k=Lyssa-ann+clarke&i=stripbooks&ref=nb_sb_noss_2

# CHAPTER 3 – THE ENCOUNTER

*Ephesians 6:5*

**Slaves obey your earthly masters with fear and trembling.**

In an attempt to demonstrate happenings in the realm and how planet earth is impacted by the unseen world, the Dragon Slayer, a warrior from the Kingdom of Light received a special training assignment on Paradise Isle.

The assignment was an introduction to community problem solving and national development. It was a case of planning for the future through tracing the past. It entailed historical research for matters of a spiritual nature that was important to God. The matters of the past were presently impacting the city of Paradise and would also impact the city's future if they were not addressed.

The Dragon Slayer was not told by the King that she had to go on this particular mission. Instead he waited until she was on site that he allowed some things to unfold.

The King was concerned about his little island Paradise and was grieved because of the ignorance of his people to the things that sought to destroy His Kingdom and the beautiful land that He had provided on planet earth for man to occupy.

Oppression had been a longstanding problem on the island caused by the lack of love for others. If the Children of Light trust, obey God and choose to hold on to the King's gift of love and take a stand against oppression the enemy would find it very difficult to penetrate the homes, temples, bodies and communities given to man as blessings.

Open doors or access points of entry would be limited and there would be more peace on earth in the natural and spiritual dimensions.

The natives of Paradise Isle needed some blessings. They were seeking change.

The King decided to bless the people after suffering for so many years. He wanted to give them treasures in growth and development infrastructural, educational, spiritual and otherwise.

The Human capital needed to be properly harnessed to ensure that the true nature's beauty could come forth on the little city that was surrounded by mountains and rivers and fine jewels was being provided.

There was just one little problem that hindered God's plan. A problem no one knew about. One that had to be solved only by a team of specialists who were designed and purposed by the source for unusual projects and missions that were uncommon and impossible for the ordinary mortal or even minister to manage.

It took a lot of faith, tenacity, fortitude, obedience, trust, fear of God over that of the critics, love for God and nation, selflessness, open-mindedness, willpower, hope, assertion, spiritual gifts, and the awesome power of the anointing to do the necessary job.

The team in the natural were considered by the nobles as rejects as they did not have a high social status, they had no wealth, were not formal leaders in the city and their spiritual gifts were under appreciated. Yet, the great one, the omnipotent Source and the rest of his team the Advisor and the King saw the *least in the city as great and the most suitable candidates for the mission and spiritual tests* that they had to endure during the initial six month challenge and training programme in community spiritual warfare

**The Surprise**

The Dragon Slayer on a visit to Paradise Isle's Memorial Garden met with two prophets at a social event. The event was held on the property that the folklore mentioned was received from the slave master in the 1800's.

The Dragon Slayer was being trained by The Advisor a part of the one true and living God. He is a teacher and the distributor of gifts for the King and his father The Source.

The Dragon Slayer began to grow in the spirit. She would detect spiritual presences although she often wasn't sure of the kind of presence until the Advisor would inform who it was. There was a point when she thought she was having information overload because of the magnitude of information that was being provided to her for the missions. When she thought that the mission was to just showcase the history of the city, The Advisor and the King revealed much more than she had expected.

While at the garden, the Dragon Slayer planted a rose bush and chatted with her two friends the Seer and the Armourbearer. She suddenly felt an eerie feeling. She had never felt that way at the garden before and she has been visiting the location for almost forty years and had never had an incident.

The Seer made a funny exclamation forcing the Dragon Slayer to see what was happening. To her amazement she saw a black man in tattered khaki clothes with chains wrapped around his hands. The man was not three dimensional and was a ghost.

The ghost spoke an African type language and had a deep voice. The ghost or spirit said:

**Ghost**: *You need to pray over the garden for the spirits to get freedom so that their spirits can go off the land. This place is supposed to be sanctified for those in Light for the works of the King to be done.*

 ***You need a group to come through (warfare & deliverance team)***. *For years the people have been coming here and raising up the spirits of the lost. Don't they know that it's gonna be time for the judgement soon. We need to go, we need to go in peace.*

**The Dragon Slayer**: *My King, my God, I don't feel comfortable with this. He wants us to sanctify this place.*

**Ghost**: *Some of the same locals from here are causing the things to happen (evil happenings)* **from generations past**. *Why, why won't they let us live in peace? Why won't they leave us in peace?*

**The Dragon Slayer then said to the team:** *he says that there are some graves within the banana piece.*

**The Dragon Slayer:** *My head, my head. I am feeling intense pressure on my brain. I feel intrusion. It was a strange feeling like something was trying to impact my thought process by squeezing my brain. That's how it feels to me. It's hard to describe.*

**The Seer**: *I am seeing the spirits, many ghosts are around us. I see some British soldiers in red suits with their muskets walking around scaring the slaves.*

**The Dragon Slayer:** *They don't want to be trapped, but why don't you guys see the light? But there is no repentance in the grave, so I don't understand.*

**Ghosts**:  *We just want them (the living) to leave us alone, in peace, peace, in peace. It's already tormenting enough. It's already tormenting enough.*

**The Dragon Slayer:** *(Interpreting what was being spoken by the Ghosts to the others) He said they did not know anything about the King and that it's like they are wandering, wandering, lost, they are lost, lost, lost*

**Ghost**: *we are lost, but they (the locals) are coming to ask us to do things, **we just want to be left alone**. There are ALL SORTS of spirits here, not just slaves and British soldiers. Children, adults all over; but people who are supposed to be from the city why don't they leave us alone? Didn't they say that the things of the…enemy, whatever.. are laid up for the righteous? If they are righteous why don't they leave us alone? Why do they need our help if they are righteous?*

**The Dragon Slayer**: *because they aren't righteous! (**as she referred to the iniquity workers** who The King constantly warned were up to no good in the city.)*

*Well, my advice to you is this. Even though there is no repentance in the grave, call upon the King for help, because we cannot, we* cannot help you. We can't help you. I can only repeat what you are saying. How can we help you?

**Ghost**: Tell the people to leave us alone.

**The Dragon Slayer**: We told them! For many months and even after the casualty of war. The King had given me the same warning or rather prophetic messages. I am  now sounding like a scratched record. Persons did not believe me. Some were concerned about my mind and wondered if I was really hearing from the King.

A guest minister warned as well. It was an extremely small fraction of locals who deliberately did evil however it only took one messy hand to cause stagnation and influence happenings on in the city.

**The Dragon Slayer**:  My King, haven't you been warning the people to leave those sleeping in the garden alone?

I don't want any communication with any of you (ghosts)!  Oh God, are you authorizing me to do this?

Haven't you been telling me to tell the people to leave them alone.  **He is saying rebellion;**

*they are coming out to attack the same disobedient people.*

*(At this point the Dragon Slayer got concerned about the innocent old people and youth who are clueless about the happenings in their environment).*

**Seer**: *It's a lot of them I am seeing many demons. I'm seeing a black man with shackles.*

**The Dragon Slayer** *saw the man standing near a mango tree and exclaimed:* **Oh gosh***! He's been enslaved forever.*

**The Dragon Slayer***: oh gosh, there is nothing we can do. We are in the land of the living on the same property where you are, even though you are lost. You are in shackles because you didn't know about the King.*

*All I can say is call out to the King and say God help me and let him direct you and tell you where to go, let him direct you to the light.*

*The earth manual says yeah though I walk through the valley of the shadow of death I will fear no evil because God is with me. We cannot help you. Call out to God.*

**We will not be hosts to you nor will our generations be hosts to you; nor anyone who comes to this garden** so if you are supposed to get to a portal to take you to the next place, call out to God so he can shine the light and show you where to go.

**We cannot help you**. I didn't come here today to be a translator for anyone, so I shut you down in the mighty name of the King. My temple is the temple of the living God and we here know that this garden needs to be sanctified. **We tried already but we did it under the direction of the Advisor and if the King has not directed me to do anything today I won't.**

The King has sent his angels and his spiritual horses already. There is nothing I can do unless the King directs me to do something right now. I don't know whatever it is that is planted into the banana tree root (**the spirit was directing the Dragon Slayer to a group of banana trees. He was telling her that persons were buried there that no one knew about**).

She then said: If there is something that is planted there that is hindering these spirits from going to their point of destination I *command it cancelled now in the mighty name of the King and send the spiritual fire across this garden so that the people who are here will find their way to wherever it is that they are supposed to go.*

***The Dragon Slayer's attention then turned towards a very large tree at the back of a building in the garden****. She then said: I don't know what' happening over there? Do you see people?*

***The Seer****: I am seeing the man, a boy, a girl and I am seeing a soldier. I am seeing many things.*

***The Dragon Slayer****: What do you see near the mango tree?*

***The Seer****:  **I am seeing a well** that used to be over there. It's as though the slaves used to go there to catch water.*

***The Dragon Slayer****: I know that this is a part of the plantation. So, they went there for water between the trees.*

*The spirit is directing me towards that area (the well) and the banana trees.  I will not go anywhere unless the King authorizes me to do so. Therefore, until then I won't go anywhere.*

**The Dragon Slayer**: *(To the Slave Ghost)
Pray if you can. Just like how you reached out
to me, see if you can reach out to the King
wherever you are and say can you save me.
Show me the tunnel to go so that I can stop
wandering this place.*

**Ghost: *NO! I AM LOST.  NOTHING I CAN
DO, I AM LOST, SHACKLES!***

*(He showed again his hands before him in
shackles. In his grey looking tattered ¾ length
cut off foot pants and a matching colour shirt
which reminded me of an old Khaki suit
converted into a knee length shorts.)*

**The Dragon Slayer**: *Why all of a sudden are
you asking me and showing me this? Is it that
you realize my spiritual gift and have decided
to pay me a visit. I'm not here to help anyone
goodbye!*

*The three prophets left the garden.  They,
closed the gates, jumped in the car and sped
away. What on earth just happened? They
thought.  It's like a movie and we were stars
in the show - a 21ᵗʰ Century Ghost Show!*

As the team drove away from the garden at
approximately 4:30pm the Dragon Slayer

thought how **being a blind Child of Light can be quite detrimental**.

Ignorance to matters of the spiritual realm may not give you nightmares, but it affects us in ways that we may not understand.

**The thought of the possibility of "Spiritual Rebellion" by Ghost Slaves of the past 1800's or Demons seemed ridiculous.** However, if there is even a slight chance that this was at all possible, the team would not want to be caught off guard or caught up in the melee.

We had enough on our plates in terms of work and have become **tired of giving these disobedient locals the same warning over and over again.**

**The next day the Advisor gave a debriefing and explained that there were some critical things to be done to see the growth that the King expressed that the city needed. However, the team must first rid the property of the Ghosts (Spirits).**

That could only mean one thing. It was time to prepare for another mission. The Dragon Slayer was not enthused.

## The Mission

The King's advisor allo*wed the King to speak through him*. **The King** said: *I know you are concerned, I know you are concerned about the happenings. But I have a purpose for you.*

**The Dragon Slayer**: *God but this thing I don't understand it. What happened yesterday was just weird.*

**The King**: *I know my child, I know my child.* **There are a lot of people that you are going to help both living and dead**

*(The Dragon Slayer was bewildered when she heard this. She thought her experience of a special encounter was a one off experience but boy was she wrong).*

**The Dragon Slayer**: *I don't understand my Lord, didn't you say that* **you were gonna use me as a medium for the**. *How am I gonna help people who have already passed?*

*Why are all these people inside the garden who can't find their way out? I don't feel comfortable, I don't understand. I don't know!*

**The King**: **Fear not, Fear not! I am with you** *and I won't let any harm come to you. Fear not (repeated thrice). In order for* *your city to grow there are a lot of things that needs to be done. There is a lot of changes* **a lot of things to be done on that site**.

**The Dragon Slayer**: *So, it was a burial site!* **What!** *The entire garden property was* **a slave burial site**? *But my Lord, look how many other places in the nation that we could have said are burial sites and nothing has happened.*

**The King**: *You have to understand that this was an* **old plantation with slaves, old plantation with slaves, old plantation with slaves. A lot of things happened in former years that you guys aren't even aware of** *and most of these people didn't even know about me.*

*A LOT OF THEM ARE LOST, A LOT OF THEM ARE LOST and* **they do need to find the gateway to get out, to get off the land!**

**The Dragon Slayer**: *Why is it that they are lost? Why?*

**The King**: **UNFINISHED BUSINESS**.

**The Dragon Slayer**: *But my Lord, is it that they don't realize that they are dead? What*

kind of unfinished business could they have
(the ghosts on the premises)? Why are they in
chains and why are old British soldiers there?
All sorts of crazy stuff are happening there.

**The King**: I don't even want you to get bogged
down with all of that right now. **I will give
you the instructions as the time
progresses. What you guys did yesterday
was the start**.

**The Dragon Slayer**: My Lord the start?


**The King**: Of many things to come.

The start.  If you want to have the prosperity
that you guys so need to have in that city, **the
people who come to try to call forth those
spirits, they need to know that they are
not there.**

**These people can also see in the spiritual
realm. Just like how prophets can see
into the spiritual realm**, many of the people
in the city can see in the spiritual realm as
well **AND THEY ARE NOT OF ME**. They are
not of me. But if it is that they know that there
is nowhere to go because there is no access,

*and everything is* **shut down** *then they won't go.*

**The Dragon Slayer**: *What was the purpose of you sending your horses four month ago and saying that anyone who enters the garden to conduct witchcraft will die? I don't understand. You said that and yet people still come. I haven't heard of any death or anything happening to anybody she said.*

**The King**: *Their time will come. Their time will come. Vengeance is mine.*

*Death is usually the last resort for me. I usually would threaten.*

*Some people are stubborn, some people won't hear. I give chance to repent, I give chance to repent and then I exercise punishment.*

*I don't want you to be perturbed and scared about these things. When it is time for you to do my work I will instruct you during those times.* **Don't focus on it. Don't worry thinking that any and anything can come inside of you and take control.**
**NO!** *Yesterday you guys needed to know what was happening.* **There are some things to be discovered on that property.**

**The Dragon Slayer: What is to
be Discovered and what is the purpose of
us discovering these things**? Is it that we
need to give these people a proper burial? Why
did they come up? Do they need a proper
burial?

**The King**: The voices of some of the slaves
have been crying out because of what was
done to them by their slave masters in **THE
WELL**. Some were thrown alive in the well.

**The Dragon Slayer:** My Lord, why am I now
feeling like I want to cry.

**The King**: If there is a way for you to get
some of the history, the history of that place.

**IT IS A HISTORICAL SITE**. The atrocities, the
atrocities, the atrocities that happened to them
(the slaves) by the slave master. Backra (slave
master), backra, horrible, horrible, horrible, the
well, **THE WELL!**

**The Dragon Slayer**: My Lord, what is this
you are getting me into?

**The King**: They need to be at peace, they
need to be at peace.

**The Dragon Slayer**: *But how are they affecting the city, can't they just stay where they are and leave us alone?*

**The King**: *Not if the people are troubling them and asking them to do things. These people need to move on. They are stuck, stuck, lost, stuck.*

**The Dragon Slayer**: *My Lord, how is that?  You said when somebody transitions they go to Paradise or Hell; how do some get stuck?* **Is it Hell on earth for them**?

*The Dragon Slayer started to wonder if there are two realms co-existing in the same space on earth*

**The King**: *They are lost, lost can't find their way.* **Remember I say to die without me is to be lost?**

**(The Dragon Slayer Volume 1 will explain more on this).**

**The Dragon Slayer**: *So, does that mean that some are lost here, and some are lost in hell? How is that? I can't even reason that out. My poor brain can't even consider.*

*What you are telling me? It's like what these ghost whispering, duppy-catching people on the tv are saying is true.*

**The King: There is a lot that can happen, and OPPRESSION CAN BE BROKEN if the oppression of the slaves is remediated!**

**The Dragon Slayer***: What?*

**The King***: Justice, justice,* **there was no justice for them***!* **Some were murdered***. Some of those men you see with the muskets were working for the* **British Army. They had to kill because it was their role to kill***, but sin is sin* **and for the atrocities** *that they pulled out on the slaves* **they too got stuck. They too wanted to find their way home, back to England***, back to England, back to England!* **They need to go***!*


**The Dragon Slayer***: Lord, it was easier as a Child of Light to just praise and worship, sing and operate as normal without knowing all these things, but then here you go telling me that* **I am not the normal Child** *and that is a fact.*

**The King**: *I have purposed you to help and help you must. You must be obedient to help.* All I want is for you to prosper and to be of good health. I want your city to be elevated. I want Paradise Isle **TO NOT BE CALLED THE DUPPY (GHOST) CITY ANYMORE**!

*They need freedom, freedom, freedom and release!*

**The Dragon Slayer**: *You are saying that you will help me, you will tell me what to do and you will also send help.*

**The King**: *I will also plant some things in your mind for you to enquire about.* **Peace, peace, peace. If they get peace it will make a difference to the city**.

**The Dragon Slayer**: *So how do they (the ghosts) influence the land of the living?*

**The King**: **YOU WOULD BE SURPRISED, YOU WOULD BE SURPRISED**. *Humans generally can't see spiritual forces* **and that is why it is so important to have a spirit** *of* **discernment**.

*Because the average man can't see and can't hear, that doesn't mean that spirits do not influence what's happening here on earth.*

***They do influence especially the evil ones***. *People know how to use them.*

*The enemy, The enemy, The enemy, The enemy, The enemy,* **the DEVIL!  He is cunning, and he uses his foot soldiers to do his work**. *These people need freedom.*  **They need to get off the land they were buried without honour. They need some justice**.  *They need some justice.*

***The Dragon Slayer****: this sound like you are sending me to do a historical research. My Lord, this sounds like a historical research.*

*Where can I find this information? I will probably have to try the Institute to find information.*

***The King****: They need justice and they need to go. Continue to seek me and my Kingdom. I will give you everything you need.* **Be careful of the WITCH she knows she can't touch you.**

***The Dragon Slayer****:  Thank you God! You are truth and you are light and you are worthy to be praised.*

*How will the work be done she thought? How will the team get the British Militia to go home. After the meeting with the King she tried to see if there was any available information on militia who died in the 1800. The Dragon Slayer had visited the former barracks that now serves as a school and found out that some men who died from cholera were laid to rest on the compound. If only she could find the military records.*

*Are ghosts real? Many believe and many disbelieve.*

*Luke 24:39*

*Jesus said, see my hands and feet. For a spirit does not have flesh and bones as you see that I have.*

*Matthew 14:26: the disciples were terrified and said it is a ghost!*

# CHAPTER 4- THE PLAN

**G**od: *I know the plans I have and it is to prosper you and Paradise Isle. The city needs to be able  to utilize the resources that it has.* **The city is blessed with wood, water and hidden treasures just like the rest of the nation. YOUR City IS BLESSED. IT IS NOT CURSED.**

**You get what you want. If you see it as being cursed you get a cursed city, but if you see it as a blessed you work towards its growth and prosperity you will see its growth come to past.**

**God**: *Work with the plan, do what you must!* **Some persons may be upset with your story** *but who cares,* **it is what I want, PEOPLE NEED TO KNOW**. *We cover things up under the table all the time and that is what impact us.*

*It's (witchcraft & warfare) in our workplace, our schools, our temples, it is everywhere and man is* **blind, man is clueless as to the factors that are impacting him** *and yet still he is not helpless.  If he knows what the* *problems are he can gauge his prayer. So it's time we stop hanging our heads  in shame and take action. It doesn't make sense we just say leave the things alone (meaning ignore the topic of witchcraft, deliverance and spiritual warfare)*

***What it makes sense to do is to pray and ask directions*** *so that we know what is affecting us.  That is what we need to do,* ***eliminate, extricate, eradicate!*** *That is what we need to do* ***instead of  being fearful****. We don't talk about these things,* **WE SAY THAT IT IS NOT TRUE** *because we* **DO NOT KNOW***; when we are giving the opponents the upper hand who know that it is true because they are using it.*

## The King's Plan for the City

**The King**: *The city will see change. If it is not today it will be seen in the future but mark my word change is coming, change is coming and* ***I rather run out those who are oppressing the majority*** *THAN LET THE MAJORITY WHO ARE GOOD, WHO ARE KINDHEARTED, GET FRUSTRATED AND LEAVE.*

*Some of us have no pride. We have no civic pride, we have nothing about us. All we do is think about ourselves we are just so selfish –*

doing things like **jumping on graves and doing all sorts of incantations at nights for what purpose**.

*That isn't how I saw my city.  This isn't slavery days now. This is different times."*

*Whereas the slaves thought they did what they could because they were being oppressed by backra massa (estate owners), the people who you are fighting against (nowadays) are flesh and blood like yourself, people who make mistakes like yourselves.*

*He who thinks he is perfect and has not sinned cast the first stone.*

**TO WISH THE DEATH OR PERMANENT SUFFERING OF OTHERS IS CRUEL.** *It is cruel and there are several persons in that city that have died because of warfare, because of witchcraft, because of the heart of the wicked* **and they keep on getting away, getting away, getting away because people don't know how to pray**.

*YOUR PRAYERS ARE NOT BEING DIRECTED TO TAKING OUT THESE PEOPLE!* **It is time that you redirect your prayers so that these people come and fall on their knees,**

***fall at my feet!** Stop just praying for yourselves alone. "*

## Advice for ALL Communities

*When you pray for the community, **you better pray for those evildoers that they be turned back and brought to shame (pray psalms 35, 91 & 68** )and turn from their evil ways.*

*Pray, for me to heal your land, heal your land, heal your land. **HEALING WILL BRING THE BLESSINGS THAT YOU NEED.***

***Pray that the forces of darkness be cut down, and that light will come through.** Things grow in light, flowers grow in light not in darkness and THERE IS JUST TOO MUCH DARKNESS AROUND that is why the place look like that nobody cares.*

*You are not seeing the prosperity because persons don't care, persons lose investments, no money coming in. **Some persons have spoken evil over the area because they want to see it in ruins.** "*

***The Dragon Slayer:** We cancel that in the name of the King right now.*

*God:* **"Why would you speak against your own self and your generations to come are you fools?** *They are trampling and stifling their own selves, grandchildren and children.*

*What purpose is it to speak against the youths so that they don't grow, so that they just stay in the area like buffoons?*

**Don't you see that these young people are already being affected by the generational curses.**

*SOME OF THESE MEN (he made reference to some young men involved in witchcraft practice) who are mixed up, mixed up, mixed up and stirred up ARE BEING HAUNTED BY DEMONS!* **They need deliverance.** *What are we doing people what are we doing?* **WAKE UP?**

## Future Blessings

*Then the King said: It's a new day,* **the city will grow. Trade will start again. Visitors will come again, factories will work again, good leadership will come again.**

*And even though we know that I will be coming for my world soon, we will still occupy. You are not going to stop working for me.*

*You will do the things I need u to do until such time because you don't know the hour when the son of man cometh!*

*I will lead the way. I will be that beacon for you through the wilderness.* **I am calling some people who want to see the change right now**. *Some people who will have to be the change that the people see so that they know that they too can change.*

**Whether or not some persons want to be on board**, *change is coming, good change, watch me work. Watch people come, watch some people go.* **I am doing a religious stirring**. *Righteous judgement in this time.  The natural resources will be used to benefit my Kingdom.*

*Bless everything you put your hands on. The trees, flowers, road, speak life into it.  Into the dead place. Plant the seeds and the seeds will grow.*

*Speak life into it! This is what we will see. This is what we will speak about. We will not speak about the things that were not.*

**We will be calling it as thought as we think it is**. *Call it as though it were!*

*People will know that I am alive and I am true and that the prayers that they have been praying throughout the years may not come the way they thought it would have come but it is coming the way I want it to be. Continue to do your work and obey my voice. Continue to love your city.  So many people just get up and leave and they don't really care. Some people are just so disobedient.*

*There are also some persons yet that I haven't given the instruction yet to move but when it is time to move they will be humbled and embarrassed that they have not done the things not even to acknowledge.  But help is coming, and there will be plans, more, more, more, **I AM A King OF THE MORE**."*

***The Dragon Slayer****:*

*Hallelujah Jesus. Lord thank you. I don't know why you are doing this to me, making me so pre-occupied with this city, but I will do what is required.*

*Regardless of the fact that we DID NOT LEARN a lot of spiritual things there, you were still there with us, working with us through our weaknesses and through our ignorance and I just want you to know that we acknowledge and accept you and because of this city we got to know about you.*

**The Dragon Slayer:**

*Today the King showed me Ezra Chapter 5. I was amazed by its revelation.*

**The King:**

*I have equipped you to be victorious through all your missions. There will be some unusual and unconventional things that I will ask you to do that you won't see in the conventional temple, and I have been telling you before that unconventional times calls for unconventional things.*

***The strongholds all over, they are just very strong strongholds.*** *The enemy has gotten used to certain tactics. I will have to change my warfare strategy in these times.*

***England, England, England ,England England****. Major city, major town, major. London, London, London, London, London London, London will be  focal point.*

***There are a lot of people who need me****. said the King. They will be curious to hear you speak and **IN YOUR HISTORICAL QUEST***

<u>**SOME MYSTERIES WILL BE SOLVED THERE.**</u>

***YOU NEED TO HELP THOSE BRITISH SOLDIERS TO GET BACK HOME.***

**The Dragon Slayer:**

*What, oh my Lord that's so scary but anyway, I need to help those British soldiers, so they can get back home.*

**The King: So, they can find their place in time.** *They don't need to be on your premises, lost in Paradise. They don't need to be there.* **The work here in will be limited because of unbelief but some things will change in future** *because they will see and know by my spirit that I am the King.*

**THOSE GHOSTS! THEY NEED HELP TO GO***! There won't be anything that you will be afraid to do if you just follow my instructions you will be successful in my instructions.  I have purposed you for this season. Prophecy is being fulfilled. End times prophecy.*


**Trust & Obey**

*The Dragon Slayer's* conversations with the King got even more interesting as the days go by. It's as though the King was sending her on a mystery case. *She knows that the King and his father are* spirits who communicates with their subjects and it feels so good to be able to hear from them. She strongly **believed and trusted that the rulers would not lead her into harm's way.** The King is a life changing experience she thought as she awaited the battle instructions so the team could proceed with the mission.

# CHAPTER 5 – MISSION 1



1 Corinthians 1- MSG

[26-31] Take a good look, friends, at who you were when you got called into this life. I don't see many of "the brightest and the best" among you, not many influential, not many from high-society families. Isn't it obvious that God deliberately chose men and women that the culture overlooks and exploits and abuses, chose these "nobodies" to expose the hollow pretensions of the "somebodies"? That makes it quite clear that none of you can get by with blowing your own horn before God. Everything that we have—right thinking and right living, a clean slate and a fresh start—comes from God by way of Jesus Christ. That's why we have the saying, "If you're going to blow a horn, blow a trumpet for God."

## A Little Encouragement

Before entering into battle the first step is to know your enemies. Where are they from who are they, how big is their team?

The King's Advisor had revealed some time ago the name of the ruler who had placed himself over the city. His residence was also known as he was the ruler of the 8th Gate of Hell.

His team was large, he had legions at his disposal as well as Pharaoh, Death the

Gatekeeper, Militia soldiers and other agents at his disposal.

It was time to get ready for the second mission. Ready or not it was time. The King proceeded to motivate the Dragon Slayer.

**The King**: Now is the time. I have purposed you for this time to minister to people who need to hear my word. To minister to the hopeless and the helpless, the poor and the needy and those who need healing. Now is the time.

Now is the time to heal those you love, to heal their spiritual wounds. Now is the time, now is the time for victory. Now is the time to build my city. Now is the time to learn the different tools to use to ensure that deliverance is done and to learn everything that the father wants.

**The Dragon Slayer broke out singing**: victory is ours na, na, na. Though the oppressors they may come, victory is ours.

**The King**: Whatever it is that I have purposed you for will come to pass no matter what. I have made you as chosen vessel for me. There will be a lot of release, chains will be broken and success received in the city because of the things you will do. Don't worry about the witch. She is getting what's coming to her. Little by little others will see and know. Out of their own mouths they will confess. Then we shall re-teach the city about what is acceptable. People cannot be saying that they do not know what is witchcraft.

I will give you more information on that as to what is to be taught as a lesson. So the people in the nation will know that what they have been doing is wrong. They have been walking bodies and all sorts of things.

Remember victory will be the Lords. Remember victory will be the Lords. Fear not the rulers are with you. Just speak into being whatever you need and it will be done.

### A Spiritual Lesson – Who is The Enemy?

**The Advisor** began to teach. The first name given was Mazzaziel. He is the principality of the territory. He has a throne and many creatures include flying creatures.

This dark angel brings a lot of darkness. He patrols the realm and allows darkness to enter loved ones. **Mystous** helps **Mazzaziel** to allow darkness into the lives of mortals.

This demon has taken many souls from the Kingdom. **Do not forget this name. He is the King for the 8ᵗʰ Gate**.  He also works through fornication and lust.

Another one is **Morpheus**. He is **the King of Death the Grim Reaper**. He works alongside other demons creating havoc and deception and then in the end Morpheus reaps their souls for their kingdom.

*The Dragon Slayer then saw a pit full of demonic souls trying to escape torment.*

**Daemon** is also strong and represents music controls thousands of artistes over the world. He controls their minds and they do his will, whilst the **Prince of Persia** has thousands of demons.

**Leviathan** works with pride, envy (bad mind) and jealousy, positions and wealth.

**The Seer**: The King has many angels. Even arch angels and their names are unknown.

**The Advisor: Metajohn** is an angel of knowledge. He teaches and encourages. He is also a warrior.

**The Advisor**: There are thousands of thousands of angels in the Kingdom of Light.

Orion, Uriel, Raphael, Michael are just a few. The Kingdom of Light is far greater than the Kingdom of Darkness. Remember God is The Source, the maker of all things including the Universe.

It is unfortunate that mortals have allowed the enemy free reign on planet earth. ***It is End Times and it is getting harder and harder for man to cope due to the magnitude of darkness on the land*** **and the light is necessary for spiritual growth and goodwill.**

This makes the battle for souls much harder than it really needs to be but the freewill of man combined with the hearts of man is the main problem that mortals face.

The ability to choose instead of it being purely a good thing has gone against man himself, as he continues to often make poor or bad choice, for his health, welfare, happiness and even life.

The Source loves his children and want earthlings to enjoy long life on planet earth but mortals some deliberately choose evil over light.

The King is the light of the world not the ruler of darkness.

He wants good things, love, life, light, truth. He wants prosperity and a society free from illness and diseases but because of the dark forces that mortals often invite into their atmosphere the world is not operating how it ought.

The General for the city had just returned to the territory. The team awaited him to share the revelatory experience.

They had thought that the experience with the slaves was weird but after the day's encounter they realized that they were going to have many weird days as their mission ministry had just begun.

The role of The General was an advisory one. After each mission we would debrief and replenish the team's spiritual oil at a specific location.  Upon hearing the mission summary The General gave his response to the seer.

**The General**: the next time you encounter those demons and they tell you that you are a weakling; they will see that you are not.  The King is giving you an empowerment now so that the enemy will never again say that you are a weakling.  How dare he tell you that?  Open your eyes seer.

**The Seer**: AAAH.. I am seeing greatly. I am seeing Mazzaziel. He is saying who are you. I am going to destroy you. The Dragon is now there with him, a grey haired old man and Mysteous is now telling Mazzaziel to send legions upon us.

**The General**: I am hearing it too.

**The General**: I am hearing it too. Morpheous and the other principalities are affecting the entire territory and nearby cities causing them to rise against each other. The enemy is against our progress.

**Dragon Slayer**: Today at assembly the King said that the entire assembly and the garden needed consecration. That was an eye opener.

**The General**: The word of the King says we are more than conquerors through him who love us. If the spirit say something negative just use the word on him.

**The Seer**: at the portal there was a lot of light burning demons right there on the battle field. There was a boy and girl with lots of cuts across their face laughing. A British soldier with musket was there chatting and distracting.

**Dragon Slayer**: It wasn't until the armadillo looking creature came through the portal that I felt an extremely strong force.

**The Armour Bearer**: The King has been showing me to always be prepared

**The General**: You should, to avoid casualties. Consecrate everything that you use.  Make sure you are prepared for all missions. Be careful of opposition but the King gave the mandate. When the King gives a mandate he equips and you don't have to question that.

**The Dragon Slayer**: The King was saying that the people will not understand until other nations find out about my gift because it is rare and this country is not used to it but there are so many persons with God's spirit who will call you to make presentations.

In other words, the gifted don't have any honour in his country. When it is too late the people will realise what we are doing is not fake.

**The Armour Bearer**: We just need to be careful.

**The Seer**: The King said, I didn't give you my kingdom for it to be a burden to you.  I am gifted but the things that come with this gift are difficult to manage.

*The prophets relayed the entire story including the fact that at one point the Dragon Slayer earlier in the morning entered a building and had to send fire through the entire building because it was filled with spirits. The Mission* had just begun there is *more* work to do.

### 1 Peter 5:8-10

[8] *Be alert and of sober mind. **Your enemy the devil** prowls around like a roaring lion looking for someone to devour. [9] Resist him, standing firm in the faith, because you know that the family of believers throughout the world is undergoing the same kind of sufferings.*

[10] *And the God of all grace, who called you to his eternal glory in Christ, after you have suffered a little while, will himself restore you and make you strong, firm and steadfast.*

# CHAPTER 6- PREPARATION TIME

## Mission 1-The Visitation

Three days before the mission the instructions came. We went into the city because the Lord had revealed that it was time for the mission. At the city gardens the Force was very strong. The team consecrated themselves and prayed.

**The King's Advisor Spoke:** The forces of darkness are prevalent over here where the slaves were buried.

**The Dragon Slayer:** where was the well?

**Seer:** The well was here, right there at that spot.

**The Dragon Slayer**: so a grave is there and we didn't know how then will we prove our findings?

**The Advisor**: Fear not I am with you Go and Look!

**The Armourbearer**: the blood of The King!

Two cats came and stood by her and the Dragon Slayer legs and purred.

**The Dragon Slayer**: *these cats too friendly. Go and find your resting place* she said to the cats.

**The Dragon Slayer**: *there were graves placed over the well* so *now* my Lord what are we gonna do?

**The Advisor: pray, pray, that they get off the land**

The Dragon Slayer did as instructed and proceeded in prayer: Heavenly father we come before you today we give you thanks. We worship you and magnify your name.

To the Kings of kings and Lord of lords, conquering lion of the tribe of Judah; through you we can do anything.

Right now I ask that you cover us, our families and protect us from any backlash as we go forth to do your work. Give us the words to say right now so that your work will be done.

**We know that whosoever the King has set free is free indeed and right now you are saying that these people need freedom in the name of the King.**

The warrior then made some declarations in a foreign language then returned to speaking English.

We declare right now that all the spirits that are here, unsettled, who are bounded and chained up we declare that you will get **your freedom so that you can go through the portal to the place where you are supposed to go. We here declare that justice will be served and <u>you will be recognised</u>.**

<u>We declare that this place will be deemed a heritage site and that people will know that you were unfairly treated and buried within the well.</u>

*At this point the presence of other beings in the garden grew stronger.*

We will find the history and will let the people know that this plantation here had some wicked slave masters.

We will declare all the owners of this plantation. We say that there is no need for you to be on this property so we say right now that you need to go!

Men, women, boys, girls; all slaves go and find rest. Get off the property now and do not come back in the mighty name of the King!

Militia, you soldier, I direct you now to go back to England. There is the road, go back through the stony hills, go on a ship and go back to England you are not needed here.

These people are no longer bounded in slavery. Slavery ended in 1834 it is now 2018 there is no need for you to be here **so you need to go back** to England now in the name of the King.

**We consecrate the entire property now in the name of the King.**

**Fire of the living God, burn through everything here that is not of you now** because we know the people who are yours are with the King in Paradise. Every altar that has been built we send the sledgehammer and the axe of the King to break up every and chop down everything planted and all altars built  the mighty name of our Lord.

We say freedom in the mighty name of the King. The land will be free from every spirit, ghost or Duppy. No more shall return in the mighty name of the King. This is our declaration.

**The Dragon Slayer**: What else do you want me to do my Lord? What do you see Seer? We declare no more slaves shall you be hurt.  Go through the portal.

**The Dragon Slayer:** Something is behind me. Who is behind me?

**Seer**: two children, a boy and a girl.

**Dragon Slayer**: I am hearing that they were sick. I heard cholera.  What is it that you want? I don't plan on engaging anyone today.

Why were we sent here when there is no water to consecrate the garden?.

**The Advisor**: you are already doing what you are supposed to do. Declaring freedom and clearing.

The dragon layer started to sing a song in an African language. It was hard to spell the words in English however one word stood out it as zumbaye… freedom, freedom, freedom she said.

**The Dragon Slayer**: it's like I am celebrating like how old people would. What is happening now?

**Seer:** those children are not normal. They are demons. Their eyes are all black.

The Dragon slayer called upon the angels to assist with the mission.

**Seer:** They were abused they have cuts all over their faces.

**Dragon Slayer:** right now it is not for us to know who is good from who is evil because the issue is folks are asking them to do things. I asked the Advisor what is preventing the slaves from going and I am awaiting a response.

**The Armour Bearer at this time poured some consecrated olive oil on sections of the battlefield.**

**Dragon slayer:** where are the angels?

**Seer:** I am not seeing any

**Dragon Slayer:** the Advisor said this is not their battle. This is something that humans must do, but do not worry we are not alone.

**We were then instructed to move to a concreted section of the property where an altar was erected five months prior and to turn around.**

**Seer:** This was an altar

**Dragon Slayer:** the place is bushy. I am not going in the bush. What do you want me to do my Lord?

**She then turned around and noticed that the rose bush she had planted a month before had not died. As she bent to care for the flower the Armour Bearer poured oil on the altar. This awakened the Gatekeeper of the portal that was erected on the property.**

**The Seer:** I am seeing a demon in an armour.

**Dragon slayer:** what kind of armour how does it look.

**The seer:** He has the face of a pig and the tail of a lizard.

The Demon that guarded this section of the gate was called Mysteous.

He was very old. His intent that afternoon was to scare us. Our advisors intent was to inform us.

**Dragon Slayer:** Fear not the Lord is with us. He has given his angels charge over us.

**Mysteous:** Where is your master?

**Dragon Slayer:** Our master lives inside of us!

**The Advisor:** Don't engage him!

**Dragon Slayer:** He will not distract us. Let us walk him out.

**Mysteous:** your words do not affect me.  I have lived for over two thousand years engaging in spiritual warfare living amongst you mortals from before you were born.

**Dragon Slayer**: Are you a territorial spirit for the city? How many of you are within this vicinity? How big your army?

**Seer:** He is one of the officials. Over 200 in the army.

**Dragon Slayer**: are they within the city?

**Mysteous**: The Strongholds are within the city

**Dragon Slayer**: What will it take for you and your friends to go back to Hell and leave the area?

**The Advisor**: Don't trust him

**Seer**: All the things your master is doing don't matter as The Dragon will get the glory in the end.

**Dragon Slayer**: The dragon cannot get the glory as The Source made the dragon so no matter what; even if all of us here were to pass the dragon still can't get the glory as The Source made all of us.

**Seer**: There are others here like dogs

**Dragon Slayer**: Okay, since you are the territorial spirit...

She started to get stirred up. Angry perhaps.

**Dragon Slayer**: let the fire of the living King

**The Advisor**: settle. Don't engage him. He is not who you are here for.

The Armour Bearer sang and prayed.

**Mysteous**: Lies!

**Dragon Slayer**: we are here for the other spirits who are not settled. Those you took all those years ago and held in bondage. We are not here for you.

**Mysteous**: That's why my master has so many youths in the area.

**Mysteous**: I shall use your sister and devour her.

**Dragon Slayer**: The Dragon is a liar! We are covered under the blood of the King.

**Mysteous**: Your words don't hurt me. I fight any battle.  I even fought Elijah.

**Dragon Slayer**: So what are you doing here in the Caribbean? We shall say again we shall not engage you.  We are here for the innocent slaves.

**Mysteous**: That's why my master has the city how he wants it.

**Dragon Slayer**: How?

**Mysteous**: I shall not disclose the plans.

**Dragon Slayer**: How, how, how?

**Mysteous**: I shall destroy every living thing.

**Dragon Slayer**: We know that the fire of our King is stronger. If my Lord says that this city will stand it will!

**Mysteous**: When Elijah and I fought he left me with scars but what shall you do?

**Dragon Slayer**: I am not here to engage you! I am here to tell the slaves to go. They are to be freed. Leave the land.

We know our purpose we are not focusing on you. We know 1 Peter 5 todays lesson. We know our adversary.  He shall not devour any of our family or generation or any innocent in

the vicinity. The only people he will devour
are those who worship him and they will
come around and confess with their own
mouths what they have done.

**The Advisor**: Don't engage him don't engage
him

**Dragon Slayer**: We say to you go back to
your master right now and leave us alone in
the mighty name of the King.

We call upon the mighty arch angels to come
fight on our behalf. We trample our feet and
shake off the dust now in the name of the
King.

**Mysteous**: I will send Legions on your
family.

**Dragon Slayer**: In the mighty name of the
King, reverse that now. The dragon is a liar! I
am done speaking! Come prophets.

**Mysteous**: My sword has pierced many
angels

**Mysteous**: Weaklings

**Seer**: That demon is from the 8th gate of Hell.

**Dragon Slayer**: We will have to return with
reinforcement. I cannot believe just to let go

the slaves, that something stronger had to come and oppose the release.

**The Advisor**: Remember this is warfare don't worry

**Seer:** remember it is he who is protecting the portal.

**Dragon Slayer**: Who knows about these creatures?

**Armour Bearer**: Do the slaves look afraid of the guard and soldier?

**Seer**: They must fear him he is directly from Hell. He is a falling angel transformed.  He can't fight our arch angels. He is just mocking and touting us trying to scare us.  It would be good to see if other warriors know the names of these spirits.

**Armour Bearer**: Glad I went into worship.

**Dragon Slayer**: Anyone who comes in this place needs consecration.  She then started speaking another language. Let's leave this place she declared.

**Seer:** Raphael and Mysteous trained together to do healing.

**Dragon Slayer**: Oh my gosh, he used to heal.. oh my..

**The Advisor**: We **DO NOT HAVE PITY** on demonic spirits because their intent for us is not good.

**The Advisor:** We are proud of the team because you went to do the work today. Do not be perturbed and consider the mission unsuccessful as you are still learning. Now you know that **there is a principality at that location.**

**Seer:** The angels are worshipping the King.  Kneeling and worshipping.

The anointing was powerful at that point. A reward for obeying the King.

**Seer**: Mysteous said the Dragon beseeched him with pride and it entered him.

**Dragon Slayer**: That is how he entered the army? All of this is teaching that we will never receive from a book.

**Armour bearer**: Wow this anointing feels so good.

**Seer**: I am seeing the King on his throne.

**Dragon Slayer**: Awww.. what are you seeing

**Seer**: Mysteous was trying to gain strength.

**Dragon Slayer**: I wonder if he is one who guide the healers with contrary spirits.

**Seer**: Elijah fought this battle on Mount Sinai and received wounds. Azurel convicted his name to the Source.

**Seer:** These spirits are monitoring us in the territory.  David prayed against the Kingdom of this same demon.

**The Dragon Slayer** went into prayer asking the King for coverage from retaliation and to protect the family and persons from the creatures that comes from the portal.

**The Seer** then said: we need to know the names of the spirits affecting us.

### The Advisor's Instructions

On the way to work the Dragon Slayer picked up that something was wrong. The Advisor showed her a vision of the city Paradise. She saw a lot of warriors on the battlefield and became very concerned. She prayed and then she got a word of Knowledge from the Advisor:

**The Advisor**: I know I have given you the mandate. So many curses have come unto the people. The enemy is plotting to kill. Take that threat seriously when he said he was going to destroy the gardens. Sometimes humans don't understand what the enemy means.

The spirit of the people needs to be renewed. Some need to seek me; some need to repent. Some are destroying the nation and they don't even know what they are doing and some deliberately know.

I do not want any innocent harmed. Rally together the troops to fight. You must do intercession soon to prevent death. You must connect to the source.  Do intercession soon to prevent death. Do intercession soon to prevent death. Do intercession soon to prevent death.

The people don't even understand what they are playing with. They think they are calling forth ancestors to help them. They don't understand that demonic force that they are playing with.  Many do not believe you.

When will they believe you? When? Even if there is another casualty will they see it as a natural occurrence?  How will they look at it? My people suffer because of ignorance. If they seek me they shall find me.

**The Dragon Slayer**: what I don't understand my Lord is why do you give me these emotions with the prophetic?  You are saying Ezekiel cried and Nehemiah cried and all of these men cried because they wanted to see change and see better. But Why?

When Ezekiel went up against Jezebel it was because he wanted to see the change for the better.

My people suffer because of ignorance and stubbornness. I tell you. Principles and procedures and the doctrines of man is affecting my people.

What will they say if those creatures decide to attack them? Principles, procedures and the doctrines of man will not save them then.

Do what you must. Warn the people about impending death. Warn the people death is coming. The territory needs help.  The force is getting stronger.

The Dragon Slayer began to cry. She was saddened that there may be casualties of war in here beloved city.

**The Advisor**: we are going to have to fight. Go and pray. Get intercessors, now! Today, now!

The Dragon Slayer wailed as the Advisor spoke she was an emotional mess. She could not do anything as the burden he bore was so heavy. She therefore decide to have a meeting with the General.

**The General**: Our Lord is merciful. I think he wants the people to come back to him because he is about to move, death angels are there. He is about to strike, people need to repent.

Since you are the one who he gives the messages ask our Lord about the strategies, plots and plans of the enemy.  He normally shows me what to bind before warfare for instance bad mind, Casanova spirit, stifling and non-progressing spirits.

You must know what you are up against and every soldier has a role to play in battle.  In the Roman army, a legion had over 6000 soldiers. If these creatures are so many what is the intent?

**The Dragon Slayer**:  The intent is to stifle the territory.

**The General**: when our Lord gives a mandate he tells how it must be executed. The plan must be carried out. I hear our Lord saying he will open your eyes as to what to do.

If you enter into a zone that you ought not to persons can get possessed. Make sure everyone is covered even the family.  If the enemy cannot catch you he will attack a weaker person who is close to you.

**Dragon Slayer**: I don't even understand why this happen when he says he gave his angels charge over us.

**The General**: look at it logically the enemy will try to penetrate any breach. Angels can be there but open doors will give the enemy legal rights. ***Once there is a breach he will try to come in. Once you are into deliverance and warfare you cannot come out***.

**The Dragon Slayer**: I don't understand why my spirit got so riled up today to the point I was seeing a dagger in my hand.

I got angry and was about to fight then I had to disengage.

**The General**: Our Lord doesn't want you to be a casualty.

The intercession to find out more about the mission was a successful one. The General and The Dragon Slayer even became more encouraged when the Advisor decided to deliver some important information from the King.

## Revelations

Blessings my children. I love you.  Continue to move forward with the work.  Victory will be ours.  Continue to learn as I teach you about the kingdom. There is much to learn in this season as I build my kingdom.

Don't consider what that demon said about the Dragon's Kingdom as his kingdom can't rise against mine. Does he know about the mighty fortress that I have?

I will equip my people with knowledge, power and weapons. **I will open heaven's gates if necessary and pour the blessings needed so that the territory will see the growth**. The days of those demons are numbered.

**Mazziel** the principality must tremble at the sound of my name. He knows me, he knows the Almighty, and he knows the dungeon that I set up for him. What he tried with Elijah he will not try with you my princess.

His threat will not stand. I will destroy him and his forces in that territory. He better let the slaves go. **They are going to get off the land. That is my command. It will be done. Freedom!**

Let freedom ring. Freedom will come. That gate will be closed. That portal will be closed and it will be a new day when they see what I have in store for the city.  Time will tell.

More information will come. More information will come. Thus saith King. There is so many things that I want to show you. So many things. **I am opening up this new realm for my people**. If my people who are called by my name would just humble themselves and turn from their wicked ways, **I will hear from heaven and I will heal their land.** So many blessings I would pour out for them. So many blessings.

**The Dragon Slayer:** My Lord, my Lord, my Lord! **You interact with me different from the ordinary man**. Would I exchange this nope.

**The King:** Don't you know that I love you my child. I have been there for you from the beginning, from the beginning of time. From before you were formed in your mother's womb I knew you.

I know all my spirits, I know them. But when spirits become man, and they aren't raised in a way which is helpful, edifying, in a way where they teach people about me; spirits become weak, corrupt. Some even become dangerous. But when people teach their children about me and the fruits of love their spirits become spirits that hate darkness and they become spirits of light! Their spirits become what they are supposed to do, because of me. Because of the earth's contaminants, what happen on earth many become evil instead. So many changes, changes, changes.

**The Dragon Slayer:**  I want to know my Lord why will there be so many persons going to Hell who just don't know about you like people from Africa. If man is going to be generally wicked on earth how is he expected to know about you?

**The King: I have made it a mission for the Word to be spread across the globe, fear not about these things that you have no control over.**

There are some people who although they might have been in a different culture still had a good heart.

I will know what to do especially in the olden ages it's just unfortunate, because **when I give my word my word must stand**.

There are many things in the spirit that I can't reveal, that man won't even under-stand.  There are many things **I can't reveal because of the enemy. He has tried from time to time to try to copy and duplicate me so there are some things that must be kept a secret,** must be kept a secret, because the enemy; his intent is to become like the King. He cannot be me, but his intent is to become like me. So there are some things I can't reveal. But know this; I know my people. I always love my people.

**Those who are called by my name** I reward them, they know me, I am a just King. **Some people go prematurely because they are not equipped**, because they **don't understand the spirit realm**, because they don't know how to keep covered.

There are so many things that impact humans, that they need to learn, **but we**

**need more teachers to teach** so that man can know how to survive!

**The things of the spirit can only be taught by the spirit. The things of the flesh can be taught by flesh, but the things of the spirit must be taught by spirit!**

If man is a spirit, he needs to know how to operate as a spirit. He can't want to worship as spirit and at the same time deny everything else.

To get this information the Advisor will teach.

He will teach who are willing to hear, who are willing to learn, people like you who are open to him; who don't chastise and deny and disrespect. Who understands that my Advisor is a part of the triune, a part of the sovereignty and that he is important, he is important.

The Advisor. He is powerful, omnipotent, purposeful, loving and rewarding.

**People do not understand how my spirit work. There is the spirit on the inside and there is anointing that can come from the outside depending on the purpose,** depending on what is to be done.

**The King**: the time will come when I am going to have to reveal, much, much, much, much, more.  People are questioning and doubting who I am. **People are doubting that I am the King of Kings and the Lord of Lords.**  Watch and see what I will do. A lot of things will have to come to pass, a lot has to come to pass before the end of time. Little by little, people will see.

**The King**: I will reveal within the spirit. When it is time you will know what to do. I am the one who heals. I am the King your healer. I heal all diseases. I am the one who supply all the gifts. I am the one who is truth and light. I am the one who will get all the glory. I am the one they will testify of. I am that one. I am that person. The people will see and they will worship and they will testify that there is a Lord. There is a Living Word. They will see and know.

**The Dragon Slayer**: God you have all the glory, all the honour and all the praise.  We magnify your name our King. We thank you for your intervention this morning, for looking out for our community. We thank you for looking out for the family. (Spoke in tongues). Merciful God, merciful Saviour, hallowed be your name. (Speaking in foreign language for several minutes)

Great is thy faithfulness oh god our father. The mountains will bring you praise as well. Mighty God. I give you praise this morning. I give you praise this morning.

I pray for courage, strength, grace, favour. I have the mind of Christ, I have been washed in the blood of the lamb of God

There is power, wonder working power in the blood of the lamb. Fear not, fear not you always say to me because the Lord is with me. I know there is so many things that I need to work on.

Forgive me for any wrongs, I repent, teach me how to help those people at church. I am trying, I am trying, it is hard. I rely on you for strength.

This is a lot on my mind. A lot of people could not manage this God, to deal with this, work, family, so much, it is a lot God. But you say you are with me, you comfort me with your rod and staff and make a table before me right in the presence of my enemies, you anoint my head with oil and my cup runneth over for your namesake. My King! I shall not fear for you are with me God. You prepare my table so.. He who diggeth a pit shall lie in it.

## The Enemy's Residence

<u>Now is a time for training to learn about the spirit realm</u>. This will allow you to know the enemy and to be able to fight in the spirit realm. You are being taught about warfare. Compile the information and put in a book called **the 8th Gate of Hell.**

**There are quite a few gates**. *Know your enemy's strength and weakness.* All can be defeated by God.

Don't worry about the city. **It cannot operate as it is now.** Leave it to me: Hosea 4:6. These things happen when we allow the enemy inside our cities.

*No more crying for the adulterous nation. Judgement I say Judgement! Vengeance is mine. I will repay for what they have done to Ivy & the other innocent in generations past.* ***It is time witchcraft be rooted out of the nation. Wickedness has its rewards in Hell!***

I will shield & protect you.  You are mine. **I am teaching you to fight in a practical**

**way. In future you will face warfare and persons impacted by warfare.**

**You must remember and know what to do by my spirit**. **Take notes on the lessons learnt**.

You and the team will help many and the ministry will grow. I will reward. <u>Your intercessors are called</u>. Build my mighty army warrior of God. My Dragon Slayer!

**Fight for God the true kingdom.** See what I have stored up for you treasures in heaven and on earth.

**<u>Not many persons can handle what you are going through, but I made you a promise to sustain and fortify you</u>. You are not alone. The enemy will not overtake you. Help your family! Help your community and your nation.**

Once we are in this world there will be trials but we will overcome. We are more than conquerors through Christ Jesus who loves us. No matter what challenge or adversity may come I will be victorious as I stand on the promises of God.

No matter what is said, or what is done the righteous will receive justice. If not in this life then in the next.  So though the trials come because we are in a war and the enemy is pulling out every trick in the book (*strategies to get financial resources, computer and internet issues, negative comments, abandonment by persons you trust who you thought cared about you, the demonic attacks whether in the spiritual or though individuals and even persons thinking I am crazy because I believe in the "greater works", operate in the prophetic and have said that God speaks and that I hear from God.*) I still hold on to the fact that the King loves me and that we have a relationship. He is my friend who will never leave me he is the best thing that ever happened to me. Nothing compares to the experiences I have had through him.

I am on my training ground. I learn daily and hopefully I will learn from my mistakes especially about who to trust. The Lord showed me the mistake I made when I did not use the gift of discernment to determine who was to be in prayer with us when I took the action of faith and followed God's instruction. He took me in the spirit to a particular location and showed me what was said by whom I thought would have stood with us in faith to see the miracle God wanted on that day.

It was a season for disclosures and discoveries as apart from the territorial issues the Kingdom Builders were still meeting and doing deliverance. Had a testimony from a woman who was attacked by a marine spirit that entered her system via her navel.

The Dragon Slayer had seen the vermin looking creature with a multi-coloured looking mane not only shrieked and snapped at her like a snake during the intercession but she saw through the gift of the advisor the creature enter her system.

Apparently the individual was ill and had scheduled to a hernia surgery however after the intervention the lump at the navel had disappeared altogether and surgery was no longer necessary.

To God be the glory the good news was well received by the team. They were encouraged and the Advisor was aloe excited there was a lot of work to do but people were afraid to do the Kings work. In the interim it was time to plan for another mission.

The King does not call the qualified he qualifies the called. There is much end time work to be done. All warriors better get prepared because after the training period has ended there will be more battles even advanced warfare to contend with.

The King is the God of war and he has never lost a battle neither will he ever lose. If one is to choose a battle team choose the team whose emblem is the Lion as this team will always be victorious until the end of time.

# SLAVES IN THE 21ST CENTURY

## Mission 2 – 1830's Slaves in 2018

From the night before the mission the advisor told the Dragon Slayer to get the team together. She did not want to go and resisted even after getting an Ezekiel 3 warning from the King about blood being on the hand of the watchman if he is disobedient.

The Dragon Slayer was instructed to complete the mission for elevation purposes as well as to assist in protecting a family member who lived in that city.

The Advisor showed the Dragon Slayer a spiritual army consisting of men on horses and commanded the warrior to fight battles globally. A little later that day he instructed the warrior to read Ezekiel 6 and declared doom for the mountains of Paradise.

He then gave an open vision of a tall and handsome man dressed in Middle Eastern clothes and of that descent. He had silver hair with a beard much longer than the hair on his head.  The man put his foot up on a rock. He had a staff with a shepherds hook.  The Dragon Slayer was curious and asked who it was. The Advisor responded *"the leader of the Israelites."* The man was Moses and he looked nothing like the popular Ten Commandment film. He was far more handsome and muscular like a fighter and he was not very old, middle aged perhaps.

Instructions were given for the Dragon Slayer to wear black and the Armour bearer white. No reason was given for that particular instruction.

The Advisor told the Dragon Slayer to get a rod for the day's mission.  It appeared to be a grand event and we were all nervous. It's only natural that we would be after we had gotten that threat from the armadillo like creature. After all, the warriors were all human.

It turned out that they feared God more than the demon therefore they prepared through consecration, deliverance, communion and covered themselves with  olive oil, had water and proceeded in prayer.  They also came in agreement with the purpose of the mission and were in one accord.

While praying, the team realized that they had unwelcomed company. They were a pack of Pharaoh hound dogs who were monitoring agents for Pharaoh an oppressive spirit that worked alongside the ruler of the 8th gate and other principalities to form a stronghold in the city. A portal for the gate was placed right over the main altar erected on the battlefield.

The stronghold had a powerful army. Its team included Mazzaziel, the King of the 8th gate, and his colleagues, Ashtoreth & Amolech (child sacrifice, abortion, perversion, homosexuality, prostitution, idol worship )

Pharaoh (oppression, suffering and stagnancy), Jezebel (wickedness), Morpheous (the grim reaper–death)

The enemy in spiritual warfare is not visible to the naked eye. They hide behind mortals, possess and oppress people, affect communities and impact progress. Our enemies include principalities and powers rulers in high place and spiritual wickedness.

To protect ourselves as children of light we put on our armour according to Ephesians 6. This was no joke. It is an invisible armour and it is very effective.

The team was not alone. There were foot soldiers and horsemen. Many of the soldiers were of Asian descent. Samurai's they were, and they were backed up by angels. The job was pretty simple, to pray, worship and most importantly follow the advice of the Advisor.  It was time for battle

The battle song was sung and the Dragon Slayer lifted her sword and hailed the King. She asked for power from the King and declared that the spirit of fear will not impact the team on the mission and declared victory over the oppressors.

**Dragon Slayer**: Thus says the King. Today is the day of freedom for those in bondage.  I have sent forth my mighty army.

**Seer**: Angels are around. I see five. Uriel is on his horse, Michael, Orion & Gabriel.

**Dragon Slayer**: now is the time for us to do the Kings work. A city divided cannot stand. You our King are our fortress and strength. Jehovah Gibbor, mighty warrior, strong in battle. Give us today our daily bread and empower us with the sweet anointing needed to do your work. Protect our family from any backlash or attack as we go forth in battle.

The mission lasted approximately one hour

**Dragon Slayer**: Today Is the day of freedom. We are here to tell the slaves to go and to tell Pharaoh to let the people go! Let my people go, says the King.

**Dragon Slayer**: The enemy tried to put fear on us as a weapon.

**The Seer**: The enemy is reminding me of all my sins.

**The Advisor:** Tell the slaves to go.

We went into the bushes and proceeded

**Dragon Slayer**: today is the day that you are going to leave this land to go to the promise land. We are here to say that Pharaoh has no choice, because of the plagues that the King will send on him and his agents. Pharaoh you have no choice but to let the slaves go.

Slaves take your things and get off the land. Get off the land. Get off the land. Today is the day of freedom get off the land. Freedom come. Pharaoh will no longer have a hold over your life.

We command the angels and warriors of God to go through with the cleansing. We await your instructions our King.

Mazzaziel! Today is the day that you will let the slaves go. Your plans for the destruction of the city will not stand. The plans will not stand. You will let them go in peace without any retaliation. You Mazzaziel know that vengeance is the King's. You know the dungeon that he has. Don't let me lock you up from now says the King. Let them go. Let there be peace on this land. There are so many other people who want you. Let them go. They have been in bondage too long.

**The Seer**: He is saying you fools!

**Dragon Slayer**: Follow the instructions of the King! I am his vessel. The King has declared that you will let the slaves go. He has prepared a dungeon for you he would you rather you get your freedom to stay where you are right now than to be locked up early for an eternity!

Just let them go let them go. You can still reign from the $8^{th}$ gate but not from here

**The Seer**: I am seeing a one eyed giant a Cyclops. You know, it like we walked in on an ambush.

The Dragon Slayer got nervous. She started to pray calling on the fire and presence of

God. She was told he is already here. She felt her heart racing as if she would go into panic mode. Michael she called out. Do the work. Our work is done. Angels, Gabriel, the troopers, do the work now! Now, now!

**The Seer**: The dragon is here now.

**The Dragon Slayer**: sword of the spirit of the King we call upon you right now to cut through everything that is not of the King. I send the javelin of the King to impale and the axe of the spirit to chop through every force. I send the dagger to the throat right now, I send the sledgehammer to hit the head right now.

Weapons were flying left right and centre. Angels were fighting demons. Every altar erected here is destroyed now!

**The Seer**: I am seeing a man on a horse body with a spear. So many creatures!

**The Dragon Slayer**: mighty army of the King arise.

**The Advisor**: Be still now. I'll give the commands to the angels.

**The Dragon Slayer**: fire of the King burn! Today is the day of cleansing...

*The Dragon Slayer forgot about the instructions to be still. She made declarations in a foreign language as the armour bearer sang. Suddenly the Dragon Slayer felt a strong force behind her. It was the Cyclops he stood behind the team, but he could not touch them as the King had protected them with an invisible shield.*

**Dragon Slayer**: we say slaves, take up yourself and leave, one by one two by two.

At this point some slaves emerged from the bushes. It was a large group. Some had bundles on a stick. There were men, women, and children. The Dragon Slayer made note of a pregnant woman in a polka dot looking dress.

**Dragon Slayer**: walk toward the light, walk toward the light. Are you guys also seeing the slaves?

**The Seer**: I am seeing a woman holding her belly.

**Dragon Slayer**: I am seeing a group filing out with things in hand. Come on guys go towards the light. Pharaoh, let the people go so you can enjoy your freedom. Too long too long, the land needs to be cleansed.

**The Seer**: the battle is fierce. The angels are fighting the horseman with the spear, the Cyclops, dragon and other creatures. Even angels are being thrown down

**The Advisor**: Michael is handling it.

**The Seer**: there are a lot of people here

**Dragon Slayer**: I am not seeing where the slaves are going:

**The Seer**: Mazziel is saying why didn't our master tell us that he is not easily defeated.

**Dragon Slayer**: now isn't the time for fighting just let the people go. You will have other territories not here.

**The Seer**: there is a giant over us. The team laughed.

**The Armourbearer**: still keep up the praise

*The Dragon Slayer started singing an African song: victory is won, this is the day of freedom, victory Is won.*

**Dragon Slayer**: Mazzaziel is calling us a bunch of fools. I don't care what you think Mazzaziel she replied and continued singing. Send in the infantry, she ordered.

**The Seer:** he is doing everything to affect my mind.

**Dragon Slayer**: keep saying - I have the mind of the King. She then continued singing. Pack up your things and go slaves.. this the day of freedom!

**The Seer**: Mazzaziel is saying that we need to pack up and leave. You forget we destroyed his altar.

He wants to fight. Do you think he wants to play? First in my life I am seeing a giant.

**Dragon Slayer**: while laughing. We must continue in faith knowing that the King equipped us for battle. Seer look this way don't be distracted.

**The Seer**: I must look, something just landed he said and chuckled.

**The Armourbearer**: we must focus so that our concentration isn't broken.

**The Dragon Slayer** resumed singing. This is the day of Jubilee she said, as she broke out into an African dialect song.

**The Seer**: you know you are gonna have to write a book about this. Man, you are brave. I am seeing more things rising up.

**Dragon Slayer**: we are not here to fight anybody. We are just here to say – and then she broke out singing rooko shanda. This the day of Jubilee, the day the King has chosen to give freedom!

**The Seer**: so, the dragon is the ruler of the Kingdom of Darkness.

**The Armourbearer**: let us sing this is the day that or Lord has made.

**The Seer**: I need a sword to chop that demon.

**Dragon Slayer**: don't engage, don't engage. unless we feel threatened. Now isn't the time. We need to save our energy.

**The Seer:** The giant is trying to touch you ladies. I only see these things in movies.

**The Armourbearer**: everything we see in movies is real and happens in the spirit.

**The Advisor**: don't lose focus. The angels need the praise to continue the battle.

**Dragon Slayer**: let's start singing. We bring a sacrifice of praise into the house of the King.

**The Seer**: I am hearing that Uriel is injured. no that's impossible!

The Armourbearer then offered prayers for all wounded in battle to be healed.

**The Seer**: Oh my gosh, where did those big dogs come from? Mercy!

**Dragon Slayer**: The slaves are leaving are you seeing them?

**The Seer**: slaves! I man not looking at them I am looking at the other creatures including the soldier.

**The Armourbearer**: if you don't see where they went then that mean they have gone into another dimension then.

**The Advisor**: It is not finished. The King is our light we do not fear. If you were to see some of the thing that come into your homes at night....

**The Seer**: I just see an angel fall from the sky and his sword got stuck in the ground. He is still here although he doesn't appear injured.

**The Dragon Slayer**: Raphael, come and heal the injured. I am full of Goosebumps.

*The Dragon Slayer then sang We place you on the highest mountain.*

*as the armour bearer prayed.*

**The Seer**: This warfare tough. The angels are stabbing the creatures, he chuckled.

**Dragon Slayer**: what a mighty God we serve.

*The Armourbearer joined in the song.*

**Dragon Slayer**: I am seeing mommy. She is encouraging me. What a mighty God we serve. She says remember the different ways to fight. **Praise is one**.

The Dragon Slayer's mother was a former praise and worship leader and official in the city. She became a casualty of war and was honoured by the King earlier that year. It was interesting to see her there giving encouragement on the battlefield.

The Dragon Slayer then described some wolf looking creatures before singing the song rise up. She then sent fire to the nearby building as she saw flying demons perched in the ceiling and on the outer edge of the roof. She raised another song –victory is mine, victory is mine, victory today is mine!

The seer laughed and exclaimed. You really don't want to engage them eeh.

**Dragon Slayer**: I have been hearing this song come into my spirit and I think it relates to the mission. It is by the rivers of Babylon.

*As the team sung the song the Dragon Slayer commented that the slaves should sing the Lord's song and leave the city*.

The seer was distracted. He was mesmerized. He said the force is decreasing.

**Dragon Slayer**: Mommy is encouraging us to sing. They then changed to a local spiritual warrior song then another in a foreign language.

**The Seer**: the atmosphere is better. I am not seeing the creatures like before.

**The Advisor**: wait.

**The Dragon Slayer**: I am still feeling something behind me

**The Seer**: the Source is saying that there are many worshipping the forces of darkness globally. The force is also trying to keep his sheep captive but I the King shall destroy all wicked. They try to change my laws but my covenant stands tall above all. Destruction!

**The Dragon Slayer**: That's what he means by Ezekiel 6

**The Seer**: My people are not following my word and are allowing pride to creep in.

**The Dragon Slayer:** iniquity has come into the flock. What else are we expected to do apart from setting the captives free our Lord?

**The Seer**: he says don't worry about it. I will do the rest.

# LESSON SUMMARY

**The Dragon Slayer**: Do we have his permission to leave?

The Advisor is saying that he will destroy all evil in the community. Is today the beginning?

**Lessons**

The Seer: stay in the Word. Read Ezekiel 23. Ezekiel 23:1-16.

The scriptures noted used personification to describe the acts done by two nations Jerusalem (Judah) and Samaria. The nations were given names Samaria (Aholah) and Jerusalem (Aholibah). The chapters described the cities as the Children of the King. Samaria first defiled themselves with their neighbours the Assyrians.

Judah also became defiled with the Assyrians, Babylonians, Egyptians therefore they were to be punished therefore Ezekiel 23:28-35 was a warning to the disobedient children of God the Source.

The following verse (verse 33) speaks of desolation) consequences of disobedience (verse 35) The offences (verse 37-45) judgement (verse 46) and the punishment (verses 47-49).

While the angels fought, the warriors read the scriptures trying to see what the advisor was trying to teach that day. The parable of the two sisters was interesting. They were then directed to St. John 4:8 the story of the woman of Samaria the well where Jesus came asked the woman for a drink of water.

Although Jesus's disciples had gone into the city, Jesus did not have to ask the woman for water he could have gotten it himself, especially since the Jews had no dealings with the Samaritans.

There were relatives of the Jews in Samaria as Jacob had bought a piece of land from the children of Hamor according to Genesis 33:18-20.

A remnant of the Jews had disobeyed the Laws of the Source regarding intermarriage and this led to the Samaritans worshipping Foreign Gods on Mount Gerizim.

The laws in those days prohibited a lot of things including what was eaten and who to marry because it would contribute to defilement and affecting holiness. Obedience was better than sacrifice. The Jews in Jerusalem also saw holiness as being related to cleanliness according to the Mosaic law. However, they still sinned in other ways particularly in acts of love, which the Messiah expressed was the greatest commandment.

Imagine if the disciples had seen the Messiah, the king of the Jews assisting a member of the enemy's camp. Their absence was a convenient time for the Messiah to show himself to other family members especially those who were awaiting the Messiah.

The scriptures spoke to the close relation of the two cities and likened them to two sisters who were not faithful to their husbandman.

The scripture showed that the people who were chosen were busy focusing on different things be it other gods, foreign women, foreign culture, the law and had forgotten their first love The Source.

Yet here in the story there was this one woman who was thirsty at the well, who needed help herself, and yet the long awaited King chose to ask her for water. She somehow recognised that the Messiah was different from the usual Jews and asked if he was greater than father Jacob who gave the well.

The King told the woman that the water he had was better as she would never thirst again. The woman told Jesus that she wanted his living water.

She realised and declared that the King was also a prophet and with this statement the Samaritan woman spoke about place of worship.

The reality was that most Jews recognize Jerusalem as the place of worship whilst her forefathers worshipped at the mountain where Jacob had built in Samaria. **The King  in his wisdom told the woman that in future places of worship will not matter as the Source seek persons who are willing to worship him in Spirit and in Truth** not in the flesh as he is a spirit.

The woman said that there was a messiah that was to come to tell of all these spiritual things that they knew not of and the King revealed that he was the long awaited Messiah.

We then connected St. John 4:8 to the next verse given by the Advisor - Matthew 5:8 which read " *those who hunger and thirst after righteousness sake shall see God*".

The three of us wondered how does Matthew 5:8 related to John 4:8.

**The Advisor**:  *Read very carefully*

**Dragon Slayer**: *his disciples went into the city to buy meat.*

The team did not see the connection right away. They were still on the battlefield and became more puzzled. It was later on that the Dragon Slayer realised that John 4:8 had nothing to do with meat it had to do with the King being alone. **Opportunity and blessing comes when one gets to be alone with the King.**

The woman at the well was expecting at some point to see the Messiah. **She knew not the time that would happen but when she least expect it she was stuck at this place waiting for her buckets to be filled** when the Messiah who could provide "*Living*

118

*Water*" showed up as she waited, thirsty, with her empty bucket at the well.

While the team stood in the circle at a place that is considered to be defiled (the battle field) as they awaited instructions, **they got an opportunity to see God the Source, God the King and God the Advisor at work.**

They saw how **prayer and praise propels angels to fight**. They saw where the Advisor aided with instructions and that **miracles** happen in that the slaves came out of the bushes and walked towards light into a portal and disappeared. They saw that **the King protected his warriors** and that **obedience, trust, faith, hope are keys in warfare just as they are keys to the Kingdom of Light**. With keys access is granted and doors are opened.

The team had to really **love** their city and **trust & obeyed** their King to take the risk of engaging in battle with principalities, powers and spiritual wickedness in high places.

They had **hope** that the city would grow that there would not be any more casualty of war. They believed (**faith**) in the promises of good and that light is more powerful than darkness so that no matter what the witches and warlocks in the city did the Kingdom of Light would be triumphant.

The warriors used the Keys to the Kingdom of God that day and accessed the Kingdom of God which is within the believer. The keys is what allows open heavens, protection, deliverance, justice and victory for the Children of Light

**The Advisor**: there will be elevation after this mission. You may leave now. The angels will do the rest. You have already done your part

**The Dragon Slayer**: so obedience is better than sacrifice for each time we are obedient we are rewarded.

I don't know what the King is up to but today he demonstrated that he is in total control, in charge and has dominion over everything.

Although the force was strong it didn't matter. The group of blacks with their bundles left like an exodus they just walked and disappeared. It happened so fast I couldn't count the numbers. The King knows the figures. For there to be history there has to be a past.

We left the angels fighting so our assumption is that the hardest part of the battle has already been won because we could feel the force receding before we left.

Apparently the principality would prefer to maintain his freedom so although he threatened us he did not want to be locked up; but will he let go of his territory so easily?

Let us hail the King and give him glory and praise for he is good and his mercy endures forever.

## The Need For a Deliverer

The Dragon Slayer had a vision. She saw persons bowing down worshipping the Source.

**The Advisor**: the new Jerusalem – behold the old has passed away the new has come. All people need is a deliverer. Like Moses in the wilderness you led his prophets in the freeing of the slaves.

***It pays to be obedient, righteous and pure in heart. It pays. Many persons do not realise that they need deliverance***. The Israelites were ungrateful people and because of them Moses did not get to see the promised land.

My beloved, there is growth to be seen and victory to be gained in this life.  I am building a mighty army with a fortress that cannot be penetrated.

The Advisor did not get to go further in to discussion that day. He however knew that the mission was not finished and he found ways to prepare the team.

*The Dragon Slayer was very excited about the mission. The very next day she visited The General to share the experience. She spoke about the mission song, using wisdom before starting the mission, not divulging the plan, confusing the enemy, the power of prayer, consecration, praise and worship.*

*She relayed the fact that she had seen the King's vast army from the night before on their horses and where the team took their position.*

*The spirits were mostly Egyptian in nature. Right at that point the Advisor appeared and spoke the word Ashtoreth. The Dragon Slayer also described the dog face looking creature that she had seen and that their aim was to keep persons in bondage.*

*The team was surprised at how organised the Kingdom of Darkness was. It was not one or two demons that controlled the territory. It was a group.*

*The General mentioned that Jehosephat had done something similar in war in that the group sung and marched during the time of battle.*

*The Dragon Slayer stated that the main demons laughed, threatened, distracted and tried to intimidate the team. It got to the point where the demon even brought up sins as a way to throw of the team and we had to be reminded that all of us have the mind of the King.*

*The team had much support even someone we all knew at one point in the flesh, who is now spirit came to encourage us. It was an amazing experience. Mythical creatures like the Horseman and Cyclops, the Pharaoh Dogs and then when we least expected it we heard good job, victory, success you guys will do a good job the Angels will do the rest.*

*We had the debriefing and expressed the difficulty we had in deciphering the message in the scriptures where the city was likened to Jerusalem in that we are a stubborn and rebellious people and he was going to do a cleansing of the land and people.*

*Fasting was also a point of discussion from the advisor as we needed to regain strength from the mission. The team then entered into worship.*

**The Advisor**: I have called you for this important mission. You have completed part not all. Though the slaves have gone off the land there is more work to be done. Now is the time for the seeds to be planted so that growth can come.

***The angels have defeated most of the demons however the main one is not defeated but that battle is not for you it will be between the spiritual realms.***

It's time for us to pray for the laziness to come off the land for eyes to be opened, for growth and a change in the heart and mind-set of the people. This will be done by the spirit and may take a couple years to see the restoration of the city.

**The Advisor**: the King says his word still stand. The people have defied me so vengeance is mine. However, I want you to speak prosperity over the city and the people.

Blessings to the team. I am proud of your obedience your rewards will be great.

**Ephesians 6:8 – God rewards people who love and work for him**.

# CHAPTER 8-THE PLAN

## Mission Number 3 – The Plans

**T**he **Advisor**: now that the slaves are gone it is time for refurbishing the city. This must be done my way. *Persons must be introduced to the Kingdom so that persons will have a safe city of refuge.*

Many will reap and mourn because of a rebellious spirit. There will be weeping and mourning. These people have killed my city with their spirits. Vengeance is mine. A lot of changes could have happened now it is. closed down, shut down.

***All my people need is a deliverer to take them out of the wilderness to help them to beat pharaoh*** but some don't even realize that they need a deliverer and deliverance. The King is the true deliverer.

For the missions, the team will have rewards on earth and in the heavens. It pays to be obedient, it pays to be righteous, it pays. **Many are called but few are chosen. How many are willing to heed the call of the King on their life and to obey my voice**.

*It they just obey and pray, I will hear from heaven and send a deliverer; but as usual like the Israelites who were ungrateful the people called and asked for freedom and when the deliverer came what did they do to Moses?*

*They cursed him and said better they stayed in Egypt because Pharaoh provided and you will realise that it is very difficult to please people. People don't even know what they want. They think that they are going to go through life without any stress, without any trials, without any pressure. Without anything that will test their knowledge for them to be appreciative about when they have excelled.*

*People are genuinely lazy and want to get good without working for it. Moses was forced to lead this ungrateful people and because of it he did not get to see the promise land because he was passionate about them he got angry and struck the rock but he was my friend.*

*Continue to heed my voice. Do the things that I tell you to do. My beloved before you were formed I knew you. You are mine. Fear not. Don't worry about what the people say or do. Hold on to my word it will guide you. I will always lead you to the truth which is freedom. It sets people free.*

*I have promised you growth. You will see the victory in your life for the city. There is much work to do.*

## The New Mission

**The Dragon Slayer**: My King, the adventures were really draining. I know you had said that Mazziel was not removed from the land but what I don't understand is why is the Red Coat Militia still in the city?

**The Advisor**: I have given you the provisions to take care of these missions. The Demons are relentless.

**Dragon Slayer**: How then are they managing without the slaves? I thought most of them were gone.

**The Advisor**: Not when you still have people from the city trying to raise up familiars to get things done. They are demons and demons are innumerable.

Mazzaziel has lots of them at his disposal. He didn't even have to use the slaves. What he was doing was tormenting the slaves who were lost. He didn't have to work through them. **There are many demons at the 8th Gate. There are many rulers below Mazzaziel.**

**Dragon Slayer**: I know you said he has Legions but you are omnipotent and almighty, if you say don't touch shouldn't he stay away. I know the war is until the end but how is this going to go through.

**The Advisor**: The city cannot stay as it is. The foundation the city was built on had certain things that were not of me.

**Dragon Slayer**: What certain things, what covenants were made?

**The Advisor**: The demons are very powerful. **You must constantly cleanse the city.** Not until THE ENTIRE CITY CAN BE SHUT DOWN will the activities in the Kingdom of Darkness stop in that city. **Shut down**!

The leader could have even died. Take me serious. The enemy's plan is to kill steal and destroy. Not because you destroyed the majority of the army there means that they plan to sit down and lay idle.

The city needs a good leader. The current leader musts be removed as a war strategy. Let the enemy think that the city has no help.

The ruler of darkness is not omnipotent. He is not everywhere, he must send out his spies to see what's happening. The plan is to destroy and now because of the battle there is more reason for revenge.

If I did not temporarily remove the leader so he could get a break, the enemy would have killed him. **None in the city is a threat to the force yet they threatened the city**. Why wouldn't they attack the leader of the city when they wanted to attack the residents? The leader is not detecting that the city has enemies. Some dark forces have surely crept upon the nation. They must get a grip before it's too late. When eyes are on the city it makes a difference.

These things happen across the globe. People know what I am talking about. **The city will eventually become desolate**. It's grieving me. There are many who think you are their enemy; they do not understand. If only they would open their minds.

If you seek me I am able and just to give you what you want. You don't ask me for bread and I give you stone. I am not like that. I am not a liar. I can see beyond what you can see so I have to do the things in your best interests and I have to shut it down.

Many want to worship me, many loyal persons to the city who do not want to leave and are getting frustrated because of the stagnation.

There is a lot of work to do. The leader walked freely into a trap. I have promised that I will not let any innocent die. I will protect those who want to worship me. I don't want them to be permanently under spiritual oppression and bondage.

I don't want anyone to be possessed because of the attacks that are being planned. Hence, a cleansing is necessary. Help will come for the city.

## A Word to the Wise

*There are some **special techniques** to be used. The very, very, dangerous demons are old and experienced from the beginning of time some of these were my angels who went bad.*

They have experience in serious warfare. Experience with some serious witchcraft from back in the days of Pharaoh. Pharaoh Dogs are working together in groups with their plans.

131

**Dragon Slayer**: Why God? Why those spirits from Egypt?

**The Advisor**: Egyptian spirits were integral to dealing with **oppression**.

**Dragon Slayer**: Ooh that's why those Dogs were there and that demon that fought Elijah.

**The Advisor**: Pharaoh was very cruel. Very, very, cruel.

**Dragon Slayer**: but it's not like there is a particular person in the community now who has a Pharaoh spirit.

**The Advisor**: the spirit came from the slave master.

**Dragon Slayer**: The spirit of oppression came from the slave master centuries ago. What did we do a year ago with the community intervention when we saw the wrapped head woman?

**The Advisor**: you dealt with some ancestral spirits but Pharoah's spirit is not so easy to get rid of.

**Dragon Slayer**: what are you trying to tell me, we have Pharaoh, Mazzaziel and all these other spirits from the 8th Gate?

**The Advisor**: it's **AN ARMY**, an army. Note the British Red Coat Soldier. It's an army! These things were not just there for nothing. **Just as how they oppressed the slaves, they are still oppressing the community**.

Pharaoh had a vast domain 770 acres of land to work with here.

**Dragon Slayer**: why am I feeling like I want to cry God?

**The Advisor**: It's because its hurting me. All those years of struggle toil and turmoil. All those years of injustice.

*All those years those slaves wandered the land. All those years of spiritual bondage. All those years of economic failure.*

The city need's growth. Cities need growth. Break it break it. *Freedom, freedom, let freedom ring from the hill. Let freedom ring from the plains. For this plain it is time for freedom.*

The slaves are gone but the spirit of slavery is still there. **It is time to take back what the Dragon stole from you. Now is the time. Gather the troops**. I will show you what I have for you in the spiritual realm. Let

freedom reign. Shalom. I love you. Be brave
my little one.

# CHAPTER 9- **W**AR

The warfare got hotter in that the enemy decided to come after the entire team including the general. However, we were encouraged that no matter what the enemy tries, or test we receive that we would be okay.

Different strategies were used to distract the team. Illnesses, oppression, financial problems, arguments, relationship problems, distracting spirits who threatened and intimidated trying to increase fear and anxiety within and a few others were used.

At one point after denouncing fear and intimidation, the Dragon Slayer heard someone say people will hate you and then in another minute she heard *this is warfare daughter. Fight using the operations manual. Let no demon intimidate you. Remember the King is truth and light and in him no darkness can abide. You are experiencing warfare.*

The Dragon Slayer sought advice from The General who encouraged the team to ask the King to put the Word in our mouths so that we say and enquire about the right thing and discern the spirit of those we are interacting with.

**The General**: Never be afraid to ask God questions.

Identify all the demons that had control authority in the city. The territorial ones for that city had included obeah/witchcraft, laziness, theft, and violence. All open doors must be closed so that darkness will not abide.

There is not much we can do. Blessings will only come when the people in the city turn and change.

**Dragon Slayer**: I am hearing that this is a war and the demons DON'T WANT TO COME TO LIGHT. We need help. We need to do a call local and overseas for help. We don't need much time. The forces are planning retaliation. The Advisor is telling me one month. **Get help or there will be casualties**. War, war, war, death, death, death.

**The General**: the forces are always planning they won't take time out or breaks or off duty but we do and that's why the forces are prevailing. If it's one month then a lot of prayer is needed. Truth is, God wants to help the city but there are many strongholds Anyway you need rest.

**The Dragon Slayer**: I was just reminded by The Advisor that I need to pay attention to his clues and that the last time he told me urgent someone died within a month, a casualty of war. Don't let the blood be on your hand I don't want any innocent to die.

**The Dragon Slayer**: why couldn't I get a normal test in this country?

**The Advisor**: Because you are not normal!

The Dragon Slayer asked The Advisor about the spirits that were to be eliminated from the city. His response was a surprise

**The Advisor**: *Pharaoh - a leader, lust, pride, insolence, perversion, death, darkness, oppression, confusion, laziness and witchcraft.*

**The Advisor**: while I want growth, *the enemy wants revenge, death and darkness on the land.*

**The Dragon Slayer**: why haven't you told the other prophetic leaders in the city what's happening?

**The Advisor**: *different job. Different purpose and gifts. The angels WILL NEED **YOUR** HELP. I am rolling out the troops.* **No one person has what is needed it takes TEAMWORK.** These demons are <u>old and experienced</u> and **THEY ARE ANGRY BECAUSE THE SLAVES WERE FREED.** Their previous plan was to destroy the city, **<u>NOW IT'S REVENGE</u>**.

**The General**: Well the King already made a show of them openly.

**The Dragon Slayer**: We will have to invite him into this one.

**The Advisor**: No. **You have the authority like Moses**. The King is within. He gave you his powers. **Collectively you will defeat them**. I am pulling my people together. This battle is for my kingdom. **Show them what you are made of. No longer will they say you are weaklings.** There is power, wonder working power in the blood of the Lamb. The blood prevails. **Apply the blood**.

**The Dragon Slayer**: This seems to be another strategy. In the last battle we used praise like Jehosephat. **If we do not do this mission then innocent will die. How do we**

**apply the blood though?** Do we just say we apply the blood.

Another general had told us to have communion with the land. It seemed costly to us the city was also large.

There is much to think about thought the Dragon Slayer, as I was previously told that the blood is literal and spiritual so communion is important. This is both a tricky and sticky situation that we have on our hands.

## The Battlefield

The enemy continued to plot and plan for the disruption of the live of their enemies. One day The Dragon Slayer let her guard down and received the surprise of her life.

She never expected the enemy to engage her openly on the job. From the previous night she was busy seeking help to cleanse the property and to secure reinforcement for the team. She was on the phone with another remnant warrior when three unexpected visitors appeared in her office.

Mysteous (Armadillo) the gatekeeper, Morpheous (the spirit death) and Pharaoh standing beside each other in the realm was being projected into the office. The Armadillo looking creature had two huge Pharaoh dogs with him.

The ladies prayed and during this time the General arrived and he too joined in prayer.

**Mysteous asked**: Mortals what will you do to us? The Dragon Slayer prayed violently. The Gatekeeper who had a humongous standing battle axe in his hand spoke.

**Mysteous**: Mortal what will you do?

**Mysteous**: Mortal what will you do?

*He got no response.*

*The Dragon Slayer prayed in a manner like she had never prayed before aggressively in unknown language.*

**Mysteous**: we will see you on the battlefield he said, then all three turned and left the room.

This threw the dragon slayer into a tailspin. She had to do something. The warnings from the previous night had her very concerned. She needed to find out about the African pastors in the nation who could help to get the demons off the property.

In the book of Exodus, Pharaoh retaliated after he  had released the slaves. He came after them as his heart was hardened so he pursued the Israelites (Exodus 14:5-31) however, his army died as the King provided Moses with power that was greater than the other miracles.

The Dragon Slayer who is generally obedient to the voice of the Advisor at the time forgot the story of Moses where he was helped directly by the Source and proceeded to get assistance from those who she thought would help. She remembered someone she knew in another country who attended a church led by an African minister she therefore called her and received information about the local branch.

An appointment was made to see the pastor that evening. The Dragon Slayer called the team and was told by the seer that he saw an attack from a witch.
 She totally forgot the warning as well as another warning from another individual to not go anywhere the Source doesn't directly send her.  She therefore went to the night service in the urban city a strange place without her rod or

warriors especially her Armourbearer who was many miles away at the time.

The service commenced at 7pm and she was welcomed by an usher. The group worshipped while watching a telecast that was being streamed from another continent. The telecast showed a massive gathering with majority male congregation who was at the front. The women were not sitting beside their husbands. The group had what was called communion a method of consecration where wine was used to represent the blood of the king that was shed when he was sacrificed many years ago. They also had bread which symbolized the body of the King which was broken for the sake of those he loved and to ensure victory for his children.

At this point the Dragon Slayer heard a voice say take the communion.
She was hesitant at first however feasting with others who honoured the King was an expectation for Children of Light.  She therefore communed with the group and waited for the service to end.

After the service the usher came to the Dragon Slayer. They had a brief conversation where the

Dragon Slayer stated that she had an appointment to speak with the minister the usher took the Dragon Slayer to the office and asked for a briefing. The Dragon Slayer stated that she was advised to get assistance from an experienced team who knew about deliverance and that this group was recommended. The help was for a specific community that was under severe attack and additional support was needed to facilitate a cleansing and flourishing for the city.

The woman who acted as the usher took up the earth's operations manual turned to the first chapter and stated:
*"in the beginning was darkness and then there was light"*! She proceeded to use the words in earth's operation manual skewed to suit her hidden agenda of causing doubt.

The witch who was a gatekeeper did not even tell the leader that he had a visitor. She continued to speak as though she had authority stating that the King is sovereign and that there is no message he sends that the people wouldn't want to hear.

She called her husband who was an elder at the location and he came in agreement with her and said that the Dragon Slayer was god's child but was not hearing from God.  They wanted to pray with her and send teachings from their overseas congregation.

The Dragon Slayer left the location feeling confused. She forgot about the threat that happened in the morning.
 She started to doubt The Advisor and then got confused.  She left the compound and cried for about an hour on the journey home crying out to The Source and asking how could she not know the voice of the King, The Source and the Advisor. Where did she go wrong. Was she contaminated ? Was she hearing from the Kingdom of Darkness somehow without her knowledge? Did it somehow manage to infiltrate her gift of hearing?

She remembered the African woman saying god only gives peace so *if there is an urgency to get help you must be thinking that you are more sovereign than god; therefore God is not speaking. The woman also said that the King would only give acceptable messages however, **the Advisor kept saying that is a lie*** *because the Israelites were warned many times over and they disobeyed what they were told.*

The woman had also said <u>that the King or Source would not tell anyone to teach his word in the operations manual.</u> What about the commission she thought ?

*The Godhead remained silent for the remainder of the evening.*

The Dragon Slayer called on an anointed prophet who advised her that the enemy was trying to attack her mind. ***That is when she remembered the threat given earlier by the unwelcomed visitor "WE WILL SEE YOU ON THE BATTLEFIELD"*** they said.

The Dragon Slayer forgot that **THE MOST COMMON BATTLEFIELD WAS THE MIND**. It is easier to defeat the human opponent within the unseen realm than the visible as he mostly functions in the physical dimension. This situation was just a distraction as the Dragon Slayer had gotten a conference assignment that was due in two days that pertained to teachings on spiritual warfare and the enemy was trying to confuse and distract the Dragon Slayer ,the leader of the army in the city of Paradise.

The Dragon Slayer remember a past_conversation with The Advisor where it was said that because of the enemy's plots and plans people will die if the situation is not dealt with. One month was the time frame given.

The Advisor had given the Word Isaiah Chapter 6:8-13 *"Whom shall I send, and who will go for us? Then said I, Here am I; send me.*
*And he said go and tell this people, Hear ye indeed, but understand not; and see ye indeed but perceive not. "*

This word showed the difference between Moses and Isaiah in terms of attitude towards the work of the Source. While Moses made several excuses when God called him because he did not want to do the task God was calling him to do (Exodus 3:4) Isaiah on the other hand willingly volunteered to meet the need and demands of the King.

The Advisor also spoke about building a city wall as the city needed to be fortified and later the King spake:

*The Advisor: It is very crucial in these times for believers to know The Word, so they can come back and fight against the enemy who is using the same word (GOD'S WORD) as a weapon. The enemy has all sorts of people working for him and he too knows the Word.  Therefore, stand in faith trusting the God who you serve and knowing your purpose.*

*The Advisor: The Lord is equipping us at this time because he wants us to be knowledgeable, to be worthy to be approved and to remember his scriptures so we can use it on the battlefield in our mind because* **THERE ARE DIFFERENT TYPES OF WAR.**

***There are some kinds that are plain but THE ENEMY HAS SOME DIVISIVE SCHEMES some little strategies sometimes that WE DON'T EXPECT him to use.***
*I have provided for you, I have empowered you guys as a team. The enemy has even tried to attack each of you.*

**IT'S WAR TIME NOW.** *He is very vigilant seeking to devour who he can and stop who he can in This End Time Battle but it's God's plan that will* *prevail, so we need to stand strong knowing that* **He Has Called And Empowered Us** *in this season* **no matter what anyone comes with or test may come.**

**Before you engage in anything ask me to put the words in your mouth so that you will say and enquire the right things and be able to discern the spirit of the person you are interacting with.**

*If you come to me I will put the words in your mouth so that you will know what to say so that things like what happened last night won't happen again.*

**Don't be afraid to ask questions like why God, how?  Don't be afraid because I am** *USING THESE MOMENTS AS TEACHING MOMENTS FOR BELIEVERS* **so that we can see THE DIFFERENT WAYS IN WHICH THE ENEMY WORKS.**

The King then proceeded to answer all the **WHYS** asked the night before by both me and the person asking the questions:

**Why?? Why wouldn't  I send my people (believers) to help my people?** *Throughout the ages hasn't it been my servants who have helped my* *people, who have helped the oppressed, those who need to be delivered.* **Why wouldn't I send my servant to speak my Word and to let the people know what I want?**

*Why? When you guys are my chosen vessels, why,* **would I think that you want to get my glory when I am the one who sent you on assignment why?**

*These things are to cause doubts. These statements are to cause confusion and fear and mistrust.* **Why wouldn't I want to empower my children?** *Haven't I equipped you. I have equipped you with the Word. I have equipped you with my Spirit, and by the blood I shed when I made that sacrifice on the cross.* **Why wouldn't I give the people who I love responsibilities to build my Kingdom?** *Why all those whys?*

*Simple* **WHYS** *can cause you to doubt, but if you know my Word you can fight back against the whys?* **WHY?**

- *Because you are the righteousness in Christ!*
- *Why - because you are the head and not the tail.*

- *Why - because you are called and who I have called I equip.*
- *Why, because you are my servant.*
- *Why, because you make yourself available for me to use  and **I WANT TO USE MY PEOPLE**. Those are whys.*
- *Whys – because the enemy is seeking to scatter my sheep.  The enemy do not want my sheep to have a shepherd. He wants to scatter the flock.*
- *WHY WOULDN'T I SEND A DELIVER FOR MY PEOPLE? **Am I not the same God, the God of yesterday, I am also the God of today AND I WILL BE THE GOD OF FOREVER!***

*I sent Moses to deliver my people then, I sent Joshua to help. I sent Jeremiah to give many warnings, he too was punished but he was rewarded in the end.*


- *Why? **I am a God of justice that's Why!***
- *Why? I am a God of Love and if people are blind I want them to be able to see. Those are whys.*
- *Why, because people need to know that I love them, and I  look out for them and **if they are not hearing the things  from the people who are leading them, and they are  not hearing***

*personally from me they need to hear one  way or the other.*

- *Why?* **The world will soon end the war is coming to a close.**

*There are many strategies that both my Kingdom and the enemies' kingdom will employ and deploy during this time.*

- ***Why have I called you****? I called you because I knew you from before you were in your mother's womb. I knew you  from before you were born on this earth and* **I knew the   purpose that I have made you for.**
- *Why, why have I given you such a hard task?*
- *Why?* ***It's because you are special!***
- ***Why? I don't give many people these gifts****.*
- *Why – because I must have control.*
- *Why, because I have to know that I can rely on these people who I have sent out to do my missions.*
- ***Why, because these people need to have passion for  my work and passion for my people.***
- *Why – because it is not my will for any to perish but for all to come to repentance.*

*So if I have sent you to teach the word,* **YOU TEACH THE WORD** *because it is what I have called you to do.* **That is the WHY I have called you!**

*So, when the enemy comes, and he is asking the* **WHY YOU....** *tell him, - it is* **because the Lord almighty, the Lord God of host, the Lord your strong tower, the Lord your rock and your hiding place, the Lord your strength and your shield, the Lord the God of Host, the Lord your provider, the Lord the God of the much more; you tell him WHY!**

**It is because you serve an ALL POWERFUL, OMNIPOTENT God and you know your purpose! THAT IS WHY!**

*Don't let this warfare distract you from the things I have told you to do. Stand strong in my Word. Stand in me stand. Lean on the King. Lean on the Helper. Trust in me knowing that I have equipped who I have called. Trust God, trust my word. Trust that I have given you a sword. Trust that* **you are powerful because God is in you.**
*It is he (God) who gives you strength and know this:* **any of my ministers that I have sent out there, I BACK YOU AND** *I GIVE YOU AUTHORITY TO USE MY NAME AND TO DO MY WORK and*

<u>*YOU DON'T NEED ANY AUTHORITY FROM MAN*</u>*,* <u>**you just need my authority to do what I sent you to do**</u> *BECAUSE I AM YOUR LORD AND I AM YOUR GUIDE.*

*This war is not until the end.* **Once you are on this earth you will have a battle to fight.** *The war is getting more intense and many persons are getting blinded* **even by the persons who are coming to teach them the word.** <u>*Some of these people have formed cults trying to get mass followings and they are using my name saying things in my name.*</u> *My name? My name?? The glory is going to them.*

*I want to see my people free. I want to see them free from bondage. Who the son of God has set free is free indeed. I want people to walk in their purpose because many are not walking in purpose. Many of my people are lost.* *MANY OF MY PEOPLE DON'T KNOW THAT THEY HAVE A HOPE IN ME THEY DON'T KNOW THAT THEY HAVE A HOPE IN CHRIST JESUS.*

*They need to know, they need to know.* **I have called you and I have given you authority to trample on a lot of things** *and I have said it already, vengeance is mine I will repay. All these people who are misleading*

my people they better watch it. It's righteous
judgement time.

**I don't want my people to be doubting and
questioning me. You have my spirit within, stand
strong! Stand strong my warrior. Let me fortify
you.  Everything is by my spirit.** I will sound the
alarm. I will tell you when is the time. Don't worry.
My will be done.

The city will get the growth that it needs. I have
purposed you for this. Nothing is gonna stop it. You
will **help many people who do not understand me
who do not have a relationship with me,** who do
not trust me because of what they have heard from these
shepherds and what they have heard from fellow sheep.

**It's time that people realise that I am a relational
God. I build relationships.**  That is what is KEY!
**THE WORD WILL FORTIFY YOU<u>, BUT WHEN
THE WOLF COMES WITH THE WORD</u> YOU
ARE GONNA HAVE TO USE MY SPIRIT TO
DIFFERENTIATE BETWEEN WHAT IS IMPLIED
BEHIND THE MEANING OF THE WORD THAT
IS SPOKEN BY THE WOLF.**

<u>*Some people have evil intent and they use my word to mask their intent.*</u> **Woe be unto those people** *who twist my word.* **I know it's hard. I know you have a lot to do.** *This too shall pass. We will learn from the experiences. I have sent people in your life to cover you because I know you need the help. They have my spirit and* <u>**know that a lot of people will come saying that they were sent.**</u> *Discern them the wolf in sheep clothing. Blessings be on all of you my servants, great will be your rewards in heaven and on earth too.*

*I want you guys to occupy, I want you to live a prosperous healthy life that is a testimony to others that God is real, and that God provides.* **Who I call I equip.** *Don't worry.*
*Things will be done.* **Just know it's a battle and THE ENEMY IS NOT GONNA HAND OVER THINGS (HIS TERRITORY) ON A PLATE LIKE THAT.**

*Do you think the enemy is gonna hand over a city without a battle.* **These things (evil spirits) have been in the nation for centuries. They have claimed it,** *but I say now is the time. I will give the command. You will know when it is time to strike. My will be done. Victory is ours. It's already been provided. Help is on the way!*

*I've given my angels charge over you. Don't worry. Step forward in faith trusting in the God who you serve knowing that he will never leave or forsake you. I love you I love you I love you. Shalom, Shalom, Shalom, Peace, Peace, Peace, Peace.*

Before the battle the King gave the prophetess a message for the nation. It was a love warning like what was given to Jonah who ended up in the belly of a whale because he did not want to deliver the King' love message to the rebellious nation.

### Preparation Message to the Nation

This island needs a cleansing. Too many evil spirits are on my land. There are many non-performing cities that have the same problems as Paradise because of forefathers giving rights to demonic infiltration.

Righteous judgment time. I am calling for a "House Cleaning". My filthy temples need cleaning. I cannot inhabit a "dirty" house. Throw out old things. In with the new. All houses must be built on a solid foundation, not on spiritual traditions. Reverse the curse. Organizations need to know the true meaning of blessings.

I have not nor will I ever abandon my people, but I must correct what has gone wrong in this season hence I am pouring out my spirit. **If we do not handle the root cause of**

**the spiritual oppression and toxicity that has poisoned my nation, what is going to happen especially with the new/foreign spirits that are being embraced is that there will be a lot of deaths because of demonic sacrifices, altars and revenge because of war!**

Satan the dragon is building his Kingdom in these End Times. Hear my words today, August 12, 2018.  It is time for a spiritual revival.  Awake sleeping congregations. Let the light of the Lord shine on you! It is transformation time. I will move anyone who dare come in my way. Revenge is mine. I am repaying in this season. DEATH, DEATH, DEATH, DEATH!
The just shall live by faith that I will redeem in this season. Man shall not live by bread alone but on the word of God. If you seek me you shall find me. Ministers who refuse to listen, hear from me or listen to my prophets will be corrected.
Righteous judgment! If  they seek my face and turn from their wicked ways I will hear from heaven and heal their land. That is a promise.

Wake up! Wise up!  Do not perish because of ignorance. **Some of these demons that have been unleashed are quite cruel and revengeful**.  Open your eyes!! If you ask me to I will reveal.  I will show you.  Open  your eyes.  Hear my words.  I love you and it is NOT MY WILL FOR ANY TO PERISH!
**I LOVE YOU WITH AN everlasting love. Will you trust me?  Will you obey me?**

I am your God and friend. Jehovah (Lord, master – relational God); Adonai (Master over all ) Jehovah Jireh– (Your provider), your rock, shelter, hiding place. Eloheim (the Strong, creator, God), Jehovah Rapha (your healer)  Jehovah Gibbor (the Lord mighty in battle). Peace I leave with you.  Trust & obey.  Shalom.

The warning was crucial. A meeting was needed with the team today.

The Dragon Slayer headed out to work then to meet with the team. There was just one problem. Upon descending the hill upon which she lived she applied pressure to her car brake and got no response. This was an 18 month old new car.

To stop the car she had steer the car to the side of the road as she blew her horn. She then put the car in neutral then used her hand brake to allow it to come to a complete stop. It was scary especially since there was an accident two years prior with other family members coming off the same hill.

It was divine intervention that assisted the three. It was now the Dragon Slayers time. Her car was in drive but the brakes would not respond.

After the car finally stopped the Dragon Slayer who was a bit shaken asked her spouse to drive the car off the hill in case the brake failed again.

The vehicle drove perfectly fine. The driver therefore came to his own conclusions on the incident assuming that the car rolled off the hill while in reverse which would have deactivated the transmission gear.

## An Angelic Visitation

Later that day, The Dragon Slayer received an angelic visitation. It somehow was an eye opener as matters pertaining to family, the city and mission was revealed. The Angel said: *"It's righteous judgement time because the King ordered the work against iniquity (evil) workers. He has given you the job to lead the troops. **Pray and cover the family. Your brake failing was not a mistake.**"* The message was welcomed relief for the Dragon Slayer. The angel then spoke several verses from the earths manual then left.

The Dragon Slayer got a few week's rest. She also realised that the month of September would be a hectic one. The Advisor gave her some songs of encouragement including one called *Lean on his arms and Pass me not oh gentle Saviour*. The words of comfort, and assurance as well needed at the time.

That same evening the team gathered. Agents of darkness were sent to the location. The Dragon Slayer saw a very angry woman with a head of snakes who hissed at her. Her agents lined the road and one was at the doorway however none could touch the team as angels lined the road and was beside each familiar demon that covered the territory.

The agent at the door tried to scare the team but they were not shaken they prayed, spoke psalms 141 (let the wicked fall in their own nets) and prepared for the mission ahead.  The Dragon Slayer was indeed The King's deliverer. The advisor then told the team to get ready. Fast for three days then prepare to war.

The team was three days away from the new month. The Advisor began to prepare the team.  He gave the team Exodus 14: 13-16:

*"And Moses said unto the people, fear ye not, **stand still and see the salvation of the Lord, which he will shew***

*to you today; for the Egyptians whom ye have seen today, ye shall see them again no more forever.  The Lord shall fight for you , and ye shall hold your peace.*
"

Exodus 14: 16 *"And the Lord said unto Moses, wherefore criest thou unto me?* **Speak unto the children of Israel, that they go forward but lift thou up thy rod and stretch out thine hand over the sea,** *and divide it and the children of Israel shall go on dry ground through the midst of the sea. "*

The Dragon Slayer considered having a rod like Moses for the next mission. She saw the mission as a similar mission to that of Moses the deliverer. She was also concerned about something else. It was an unusually weird radiating feeling.

The Advisor: I won't let any harm come to you. I am preparing you for the supernatural mission, *and I am also teaching you history and you will get a testimony because of the demonic stance and The Source's mighty hand*. I back and empower. Remember to fast starting tomorrow. <u>**That will empower you as these demons are very old**</u>.  I am preparing you and the General like Moses and Aaron.

***Remember you have a Moses anointing***. Read Deuteronomy 7 verse 1-11 which spoke about a battle as well as the King's  love for the chosen people rewards for loving and obeying The King and punishment to those who hate the King and community growth.

**Do not take pity on people if they are evil they will not occupy**! Its prosperity we need in the city. I am cleaning spiritually. All iniquity workers must go. Justice served and deserved.

Pharaoh must let my people go. The demons shall not return. I have promised prosperity for the land. Freedom from Egypt. No more oppression.

The Advisor was teaching he even intervened in a discussion about angels and the theory that The King's true angels are only those mentioned in the operation's manual which were few.
I remembered the night I saw the two huge angels enter my bedroom one angel's sword was so long its handle touched my roof. The
Advisor  mentioned the fact that there are a lot of angels who are not mentioned in the operations manual.

Case in point the one the Dragon Slayer saw on an airplane. There are many questions only the King can answer. ***This will be done according to the Kings wishes to whom he wants in his own timing and according to the individual's purpose.***

Angels do what God authorises. While we do not worship angels we can command them to work on our behalf. Both humans and Angels must submit to the King ruler of all and the rest of the godhead.

## The Holy War

The next day the Advisor spoke about the upcoming war.  The Dragon Slayer declared that many shocking things have happened in the season but according to the Godhead we are more than overcomers.

**The Advisor**: *I have called you for this time for this season to do my work. I am getting the team ready to join you. There will be peace in the midst of the storm. **I have called the righteous not the unrighteous and who i have called I have prepared and I will equip.***

***This battle is not a normal battle.*** *It will be a little bit different from the one with the Israelites though* **the mission is the same for Pharaoh to release my people so that they can get the land, oppression can stop.**

*Continue to rely on me to strengthen you. The strategies are being laid on your heart. When the time comes for the mission I will sound the trumpet the team will know and you will assemble on the ground to fight this historical battle that will be significant to the country the land you love.*

*You will take out the Amorites the Amalekites, the Hittites. Every enemy must go who have built up territory on that land.* ***I have given them enough time to listen to me to take my warning. Iniquity workers will have a price to pay for their rebelliousness and disobedience and for the plagues they have caused on my people.***

So much hurt, death and destruction through the years because of disobedience because of rebelliousness and your dirty hands.  Oh my people who I have called and empowered; you will do a mighty work on that day. **Judgement on the enemy's camp!**

We are going into the enemy's camp and we are
taking back what they have stolen from us
throughout the generations. This has been ordered
by the almighty. The Lord, mighty in battle the
Lord our strong tower the king of glory. Victory is
says the King.

Sound the alarm.  It's war time! We are charging
forth. We are gonna be breaking down the walls of
Jericho. We are charging forth with the swords in
our hands and we are gonna be blowing our
trumpets and no force shall stand against us.

Nothing shall stand in our way. At the sound the
signal of the Lord every wall shall be torn down in
the name of The King. This is what he has
established. This is what will be done. This is what
the Lord says: (spoke in a foreign language for
quite a while).

*" we are coming against the enemy, we are coming
against the enemy, we are taking it back, we are taking
it back. Victory is ours, victory is ours. In the mighty
name of Jesus.  We praise his holy name we praise his
holy name WAR, YAHWEH,  YAHWEH, YAHWEH,*

*YAHWEH YAHWEH's holy war, YAHWEH, YAWEH, YAHWEH, this battle is for YAHWEH the holy one. Hail the King, we honour the King, the King"*

## Warning to the City

*Destruction is nigh!* **All your high places will be broken down, your idols destroyed along with your altars, Your serpent spirits will leave my land.** *You witchcraft will not save you from what* **I have planned** JUSTICE AND VENGEANCE IS THE LORDS.

*Oh ye mountains of Zion, how strong is your fortress. How far will you run when I stretch forth my mighty hand? I have warned you over and over again.* **Let my people go. Leave my people. Set them free from your oppression.**

*The indignation they have suffered due to years of oppression.*
**Years of diviners and sorcerers working to stifle their growth and success.**

**I am tired of the darkness and the shame.** *The hopelessness and helplessness of the* **people who have**

*so many resources available to them, but are*
*blind. Its time.*

***Today is the day for deliverance for the nation*** *(the*
*communities of Paradise and its environs).*
*Justice will prevail from the north, to the south, from*
*the east to the west.   The entire **770 acres of land***
*(between the stony and broad mouth rivers, extending*
*to the valley to the west of content mountain ending in*
*the above rocks region) will see change come.*

*IT'S FREEDOM TIME. IT'S TIME FOR THE*
*CURSE TO LIFT FROM OFF THE LAND.*
*VICTORY IS MINE SAITH THE LORD. JUSTICE*
*AND TRUTH WILL PREVAIL.*
*I will write the wrongs that were done centuries ago by*
*the slave master and your ancestors and break you from*
*the bondage that slavery has caused that has affected*
*many generations. That has affected your wealth and*
*prosperity.*

*I am calling from the four corners of the earth my*
*warriors who were ordained for this kind of spiritual*
*battle.*

Warn Pharaoh to let my people go! The battle is
already declared and won by the Lord God

almighty. The Lord mighty in battle. The God of Israel.

Repent evil doers, repent iniquity workers, repent obeah workers, repent community destroyers, repent!

It is not my wish for none to perish but for all to repent and have everlasting life. It's time to let go of the old, so I can heal your land! Let freedom ring from the hills and plain of Paradise. Its righteous judgement time!

**Ezekiel 6 is your portion.**

That was the preparation message given regarding the Holy War. The Dragon Slayer called the General and shared the directives.

### Warfare Instructions

**The Advisor:** Go into the **city and pray.**

**The Dragon Slayer**: *We are directed to Ezekiel 6. I was told its righteous Judgement time.* **The King said**

*to go into the community and pray as human spirits cannot fight demons.*

**The Advisor**:  The strategic direction of the prayer will change things . That is what will change things. Infused with The Word.

**The Dragon Slayer** : Pray the Words in the Earth's Manual . This is what will change things?

**The Advisor**: It's going to be a combination of PRAISE, WORSHIP, PRAYER AND SONG. **The army is large but just like how he has gathered his troops I have also gathered my troops**.

**The Dragon Slayer to the General**:  I don't know if you are seeing like me but the advisor is saying  LOOK AND SEE MY VAST ARMY! I am preparing the troops to cover the entire territory to the north, south east west. I have assigned leaders to stand guard. My Arch Angels they know what to do already and they will sound the alarm. **Once we give the orders they know what to do.**

**The Dragon Slayer**:  I am seeing some nasty looking creatures.

**The Advisor**: Don't focus on them. There is more of us than them. No matter what Pharaoh says he has to let my people go. **Remember the Rod!**

**The General**: Remember to pray first

**The Dragon Slayer**: so we are to *pray first, consecrate ourselves, carry a rod. The King will send his angels in first. There is more of us than them.*

**The Advisor** : no matter how many of his cronies Pharaoh calls he can never out do my army.

Those were great words of assurance for the entire team. Victory has already been guaranteed by the King.

# CHAPTER 10 - THE TEST

## Mission 4

*The King gave his instructions to prepare the warriors for battle. The Dragon Slayer got prepared as the "Moses the Deliverer "for this mission. The King had instructed the Dragon Slayer to let down her hair for this mission and to carry a rod.*

**The Dragon Slayer:** The King has said greater is he who is within us that he who is in the world and that he did not give us a spirit of fear but power love and a sound mind.

As we get consecrated let us remember the Kings sacrifice and that we are mere mortals and this battle is our Lord's and that we are not the one who will fight but the Lord's. He has sent his angels to fight this battle and has given his angels charge over us and to keep us in his ways. We will be obedient.

Walk boldly soldier, you're a soldier she shouted to the Seer who appeared to be very afraid. Which soldier have you seen walk the way you are walking brethren? She chuckled. Brethren walk boldly as the Lord has given you the power to trample on scorpions and serpents and everything. So what are you worrying about Prophet? Fear feeds these things stop being afraid.

On this mission the King added another prophet to the team of warriors needed to deliver the city from the hands of the enemy. Her role was a surprise to us as we had expected to also have the General with us on this mission. Another leader a shepherd was to also join the team but he did not show up. It was the team of three women and one man with the new prophetess being given the responsibility of Aaron the spokesman.

**The Dragon Slayer**: the Lord is your light and salvation who shall you fear.  The Lord is my shepherd I shall not want he maketh me to lie down in green pastures, say it…

The team recited Psalms 23 from the earth's manual.

**The Dragon Slayer**: those are promises that the King has made and the confidence he gives us his servants. We just sang that consecration song for a reason. The King said it was to prepare us for this mission.

When we consecrate ourselves, it allows the King and The Advisor to do the King's work through us.

**Prophetess**: It is me the Lord thy God do not be afraid.

**The Dragon Slayer**: He will cover us with armour. Armour – head, chest, hands, feet. She then broke out singing.

**The Dragon Slayer**: spirit of the Living God fall a fresh on me. He is here hallelujah, he is here Amen.. sing, sing, sing. He is here listen closely, you can touch him.

**The Dragon Slayer**: The Advisor is giving me so many instructions. So first, Jeremiah 12.
The Dragon Slayer made some declarations in another language then threw down the staff upon

the instruction of the Lord thy God who is the leader who will help the people to cross over the Jordan. They have already crossed over the Red Sea but Pharaoh is still chasing after them but he shall not overcome them.

You are always righteous God, said the Dragon Slayer. She then declared the words in Jeremiah Chapter 12.

**The Dragon Slayer** then said to an invisible spirit who spoke: go behind me.  This is the word of the Lord thy God and I know that you know it.

**The King**: the intent is to make my garden a desolate waste land. Take a picture of it because year from now you will see a change. It will not be like this, it will be glorious.

The Dragon Slayer completed the reading of Jeremiah 12 and said. That is the declaration of the King.

If the nation does not heed, he will destroy. No turn to **Deuteronomy 7** after reading the line that said the people were to break the enemy's altar

and burn their poles, the Dragon Slayer spoke in a
strange language and declared the poles to be
burnt.

**The Dragon Slayer**: the Lord delivered you from
the oppressions of slavery, from the power of
Pharaoh, King of Egypt.  That is what God did.
Know therefore that the Lord thy God is God he is
faithful keeping his covenants and love to a
thousand generations of those who love him and
keeps his commandments but those who hate him
he will repay to their face by destruction.

Therefore take care to follow the commands and
decrees given today.  If you follow the commands
the Lord will bless you. You will be blessed more
than any other people. None of your women and
men will be childless and the Lord will keep you
free from any disease.  He will inflict pain on all
who hate you.
You must destroy all the people the Lord give
over to you. Do not look at them with pity and do
not serve their Gods for that will be a snare to you.

Do not fear the nations.  Remember what the Lord
did to Pharaoh and Egypt he will do the same to

those you fear now. The Lord your God is an awesome God.

*The Lord will eliminate the nation before you but he won't do it all at once.* He will give their Kings under you. Do not covet their things as it is detestable to the Lord.

**The Seer**: you don't see what is happening. We are surrounded by people.

**The Dragon Slayer**:  Command the angels to do their work.  We won't pay the people you see any mind.

The Dragon Slayer  went into prayer. She drew parts of Psalms 35 and continued in prayer:

**The Dragon Slayer**:  Oh heavenly father we command the spirit of fear to go from the prophets today. Strengthen us Lord as we command Michael, Gabriel, Gersham, Nekasa, Koshebeseh, and all the Arch Angels here to line up right now.  Troops together! Men on horses, Infantry! I place you upon the four corners of this land all 770 acres of the city that was ruled by backra massa in the 1800's.

Our Source, you are the one who has declared this and has commanded the city to prosper. You said that this battle has already been won even before it has started. Put the words into our hearts so we know what to do as we go forth into battle.

**The Advisor**: before you give the command go and put the flower you had cut earlier on the memorial spot for our previously fallen soldier. The final casualty here in this city.  That is the declaration. Final casualty.


The city will be rebuilt starting from the then the other parts will be built.  What you are seeing here is desolate it has been taken over by things that has defiled it. Things have been planted under the ground from before 1904 and they will be uprooted in the spirit today as the cleansing goes throughout the entire 770 acres of land. We declare purification so that the trees, the water, the streams, the grass, every fruit, tree, living creature, in this city that they will be purified by the King.

We declare that we will have trees of righteousness, hope, forgiveness, civic pride, trees of people who want to work.

The Prophetess began speaking in an unknown tongue. She declared the blood of the King.

**The Dragon Slayer**: We declare September 11 as a new day in this city. Bad mind (envy) will end and there will be growth and prosperity will be on the land as declared in Jeremiah 29:11.

**The Dragon Slayer**: We will now honour our soldier that fell on January 31st then return to this spot.

While preparing for the mission, the Advisor had told the Dragon Slayer to pick an Orchid from the Soldier's home and to on the way over to lay the flower in memory of the exemplary leader who was lost prematurely because she was not taught how to fight in the spirit.  The team sang the blood prevailed, wonder working power in the blood.

**The Dragon Slayer**: We consecrate this water and cleanse the area of any defilement that was done here by workers of iniquity. We lay this orchid as a symbol for the growth that will come to this city. Let's go now.

**The Dragon Slayer**: Oh Lord what is this I am hearing. Oh Lord I don't think I want to go there she said.

**The King**: you will do as I say!

The Dragon Slayer proceeded to dialogue with her Lord in a language unknown to the rest of the team. She was now hearing several voices speaking and wanted to get clear instructions before proceeding.

**The Advisor**: sing the blood prevails.

The Dragon Slayer began to speak in an African type language. She spoke then interpreted.

**The Dragon  Slayer**: Ka, nan a na, Kunno, ni shi, nan a nana. Knnu nu, shi – ni, Kanna –shana. Mo-ku-to, she'ne tanya tata.  Spirit of the living God fall a fresh now upon this land.  Through the trees.

Ne-ah, ya sha-na. Some are through the trees. Neh a ha na..

It was apparent that there were now other persons apart from the prophets in the city. **I can hear a voice saying that there were some slaves left behind. I am not seeing though who is talking.**

Are you seeing them seer?
**The Dragon Slayer**: Tell me what you see Seer.

**The Seer**: I am seeing someone sitting where the well was.

**The Dragon Slayer**: Who are you?

**Slave**: Nee-Han

**The Dragon Slayer**: Nee-Han and family? He is saying we were unjustly treated by Backra Maasa. Are you seeing male or female?

**The Seer**: I am seeing a man.

**The Dragon Slayer:** Why didn't you go with the rest of the slaves in June?

**Slave:** I was afraid to go at the time but I want to go. Here is not a nice place. I want to go. Help!

**The Dragon Slayer:** you should have gone when we sent the rest off the property.

**Slave**: you don't understand, the torture the torment that these things do to us over here for years. Years of torment. We were lost walking up and down.

**We rebelled and Backra didn't like it!** He gave me punishment. He says I will never ever leave this place. I wanna go home. I wanna go home. Home to Africa, I wanna go home.

**The Dragon Slayer**: but what you are telling me isn't from the places where people came from.

**Slave:** Yurubu Kasa. Yurubu Kihasa, Yuhusha tu Ghana Kasana! I wanna go home to the land that is fairer than day. I wanna go home, home, home is where my heart is, the precious land where there are so many different creatures.

I don't like it here. Backra Massa! Ma ma ma seeka to ka-seke.  He was cruel. There were over 100 persons thrown in the well. I initially got away but he found out and ensured that I was never to rise again.  A-bba-baya. Help, Ne-ha. Help me, gu-to-see.

Help me, kushu-hu-ta. To go to be with family, ka-ty-ya.

**The Dragon Slayer**: Look and tell me what else do you see through the trees.

**Slave**: Ne-heyma. Too many years, a-maya of suffering. My family gone leave me but-i-ki-see. I wanna go.

**The Dragon Slayer**: I am feeling a stirring in my belly. I am asking the Advisor what to do. **He is saying everything must go. Oh my Lord**. Seer what are you seeing.

**The Seer**: A man with a spear in his hand.

**The Dragon Slayer**: does he look like an African? If he has a spear more than likely. What is he wearing because unlike the last time I am not seeing the slave today.

**The Seer:** he has a piece of dirty cloth around him.

**The Dragon Slayer:** does he look like the first slave in the khaki clothes. Lord why are you not allowing me to see today?

**The Advisor**: because I need you to focus. All of us have a job here to do.

**The Dragon Slayer**: it is written that man must die once and after that the judgement.
It is written that he who does not accept the King is lost. It is written that man shall not live by bread alone but by every word that comes out of the mouth of the Source. It is also written that today is your day of freedom. So like Jeremiah who was the lone voice crying in the wilderness,
like  Ezekiel who had to do some things that he considered defiling, like what's happening with me right now with these interpretation; just as how the Lord asked Ezekiel to cook over excrement. Just like Moses who was given a task

so I have been assigned with this task says the Lord Almighty –The Source.

The Lord strong and mighty in battle.  Today we declare that the power of our God is here and we declare like when Moses was in Egypt that all slaves shall be freed and we say Pharaoh, let God's people go in the name of the trinity. Let the slaves go.  You will let the people go.

Pharaoh is saying that he will not let the people go. **I am seeing a Pharaoh like in the Moses movie with the headgear**.
I don't understand because I am hearing two different spiritual names. I am hearing Molech as well.

**The Dragon Slayer**: Heavenly father today we declare that your righteousness stands and prevails and we declare that there will no longer be any disturbance in the city of Paradise. We declare that who the King has set free is free indeed. We declare that the people will rest until the day of judgement and we declare that whomever the King has assigned duties will do their work.

We declare that no enemy shall overtake this land. No enemy shall run this land. We declare as seen in Revelations 12:11 that the King defeated the enemy by the blood and testimonies. We declare that justice will reign and freedom will reign.

**The Dragon Slayer then burst into song**: let praises rise….the rest of the team joined worship. We declare today freedom upon this land and declare that there shall be no one left behind. So we say that today is your day of freedom. Today justice will prevail.

Today we say to Pharaoh let God's people go, let the slaves go today we say that as in those days of Moses so today will you let go the people who you have held in bondage. We declare that the power of our Lord will come over this Land and that he will part the waters for the slaves to go through.

We declare a safe journey and that nothing shall overtake them in the mighty name of our King and that they will get to that land to that place that the King has ordered for them. So take up your bundles.

**Prophetess**: thus saith the King, set my people free or I am going to burn down this place with fire! Fire inna mi hand, fire inna mi foot. Fire inna mi eye, fire inna all ova mi. In di name of di King! I send fire, fire, fire, fire, fire.. I see the fire, I feel the fire. Send it down and let it burn and perish them my Lord. Free who is to be freed right now, I say free, I say free.

Don't think she is no fool, I gave her the power! I say do set my people free.

After that exclamation, the prophetess ran fearlessly into the bushes with a mop stick that was symbolic of an ancient rod or staff.  This modern day Aaron had no fear speaking on the behalf of Moses. The prophetess charged past the well where the African was sitting and showed that she was not afraid nor a fool. She was brave because the King had anointed her for the mission. As a matter of fact the entire team was anointed.

The day's events were being revealed like scenes from a movie and we were a part of the show.

*Slaves in the 21ˢᵗ Century starring three prophetess and one prophet.*

**Prophetess**: I shall not be afraid she shouted to whatever it was she was seeing in the bushes.

All the other prophets were shocked at the bravery and utterance of the prophetess and she screamed and charged with her rod holding it like it was a spear or javelin.

**Prophetess**: set, my people free……Don't be afraid don't be afraid. Hold the sword and thrust the sword in his belly.  Put the sword and say this is the sword with the fire, right in your belly. Set my people free.

**The Advisor**: I rise up new people to war. Don't you ever test her. Don't look at her as a weakling because she has the power.

The rest of the team sang the blood prevailed while the proverbial Aaron did her thing in the bushes

The Dragon Slayer at this point went into warfare mode and starting firing shots into the bushes covering the prophetess who had gone after enemy. While the others sang.

**The Dragon Slayer**: stand, stand says the King. We shall stand and those of you that are hiding in the building get out now.

**Prophetess**: don't you dare intimidate him.

**The Dragon Slayer:** The fire of God goes through this entire property.

**Slave**: Neha, neh, kasa.

The Dragon Slayer pointed the rod and used it to release a lot of ammunition like that of an automatic rifle. She declared no more.. no more.

**Prophetess**: we all have a job here to do. Seer tell us where to go so we can put the sword where we should.

**The Dragon Slayer:** yes my Lord, yes my Lord. Guys, he wanted to set a trap for us.

**Prophetess:** we make a pledge we shall fight to the end.

**The Dragon Slayer:** that demon was trying to get us to go where he is to help him.

**Prophetess**: no, no, I want to go over there. I feel like I would just fly. I feel light.

**The Dragon Slayer:** everyone got a chance to go. The only reason why he didn't go was because that was a part of the enemy's plan.  He is here crying for help when he got the chance. Well, yuh feneh, because you will perish with the rest of the spirits on this property.


Lord what do you say? I spoke through my prophetess.

**Prophetess**: they are used to you people not me.

**The Dragon Slayer**: the King gave you power and authority to trample upon serpents and scorpions.

**The Dragon Slayer:** now this is what our Lord says. Today is the day of judgement. Every living creature that is here that is not supposed to be here because I did not put you here go now in the name of the trinity otherwise you will die from the Supreme's fire.

This is the day the Lord has made let us rejoice and be glad in it.

**The Dragon Slayer then broke out singing** an old negro spiritual. *Freedom, over me and before I be a slave I be buried in my grave and go home to my Lord and be free.*

No one else from this city will fall in your trap. You will not enslave any more from this city. You will not get anyone else to work for you. You will leave. Every principality and powers and strongholds established must go in the name of the King we come against witchcraft that has killed this city for generations, the generational curses because of the forefather, the blood sacrifices.

Angels of the King, Angels of God, Infantry, Artillery, men on horses charge, now! Combat..

war, war, war, war. For the Lord strong and mighty.

The King has commanded this that this battle is ordained and that it's the Lord.

Are you seeing anything? I saw the army on horses. Angels of God command the angels to fight.  The proceed to sing by the rivers of Babylon and the other songs prepared before the mission.

**The Team**: Fire, fire on the enemy, **bun dem up! Fire pon di enemy, bun dem up!** Sons of God arise!


The warriors had fun singing fire on the enemy until the Dragon Slayer heard a voice say: **WEAKLINGS!**

**The Dragon Slayer** said**: receive the fire!** The King has ordered that if Mazziel does not release this territory then he will place him in the dungeon for an eternity before his scheduled time. Thus says our King. So today Mazziel needs to make a decision to leave our territory. **Today is the day that you the rulers of the 8th Gate of Hell**

**will decide to leave the land, the community of Paradise and the people alone.**

No more casualty of war. No more shall die because of you, because of witchcraft, unexplained sicknesses, no more. Thus says our King. Desolation. Ezekiel 6 and the victory is HIS. This war has already been won.
Whether or not we see angels here the battle has already been won and we have the Moses Anointing on us and today God will part the waters jut as how he parted the waters for Moses is what the Source has declared.


People go through. Let's sing. Sons of God arise.., .fire in the hand, fire in our mouth fire in our feet, Sons of God arise, bun dem up..

The team was militant. They took position at the four cardinal points in the same positions where they had dispatched the spiritual warriors at the beginning of the mission.

**The Dragon Slayer**: the next song is Onward Christian Soldiers. Let's begin.

The prophets sang as the Dragon Slayer tracked the song making the sound of a trumpet with her mouth and held the pace of the battle song. At the second chorus she emphasised the following:

**The Dragon Slayer**: at the sight of triumph the Dragon's Legions flee, then on Christian soldiers, on to victory.

*Hell's foundation quiver at the shout of praise, brother lift your voices, loud your anthem raise.  Brothers we are not divided all one body we, one in hope and doctrine, one in charity…gates of Hell can never against the Kingdom prevail. We have the Kings promise and that cannot fail…onward soldiers..*

**The Armourbearer**: I just heard a door open did you hear it?

**The Dragon Slayer**: yes I heard the door open in the empty building. It's been happening before. She declared they have to come out.. let's go next verse.

**The Team**: glory, laud and honour to our King, men through the ages sing.

**The Dragon Slayer**: this song had a key in it hence the Advisor has been giving me the song all week. There is power in these old songs. I am also hearing the voice of the person who encouraged us the last time saying keep singing, keep singing.

Forward into battle see his banners go….

**The Dragon Slayer**: do you realise we are now at the spot where we fought the last time.

**The Seer**: we should have gone in the building to fight. That is where the enemy is seeking refuge.

**The Dragon Slayer**: we will not go anywhere we are not sent.

**The Dragon Slayer**: you can't be afraid in the open yet want to go inside a building where the enemy has his troops.

**Come on next song:** *we are marching to Zion, beautiful, beautiful, Zion, were marching upward to Zion the beautiful city of God.*

**Children of the heavenly King must speak the joys abroad…..(she then started to speak another language).**

**Prophetess:** I am seeing someone in white that I know smiling in the heavenly realms.

**The Dragon Slayer**: I am seeing angels flying around a lot of them like they are in worship and are enjoying the song.

The Advisor is saying that we now need to sing a song about thanks.

**The Team**: Thanks, we give you thanks for all you have done…we give you thanks.

The Dragon Slayer at this point while the rest of the team gave thanks, spoke in an unknown language then said: the battle is the Lord's.

Great is thy faithfulness oh the Source,  God our father.

The Armourbearer: Am I the only one who is seeing that light?

Night was at hand and the team was in the middle of the battlefield.  There was no man-made light, fire, nor was it a full moon. The natural lighting was getting poor.  The only thing that could give additional lighting was the car nearby but the team was so busy.

**The Dragon Slayer**: Hymn 555.  Mine eyes have seen the glory.

The team sung the song making trumpet sounds and all.

**The Dragon Slayer**: glory, glory, hallelujah, stretch forth your mighty hand God. Stretch for your mighty hand. Let the hero born of woman crush the serpent with his heal as our Lord marches on. Glory, glory, hallelujah.. That's the truth that the King declares today. Victory is ours.

The team raised another song about loving the King.

**The Armourbearer**: that star, the light was far away now it is so close to us. Have you noticed?

The Prophets: Oh yes its true.

**The Dragon Slayer**: I am now hearing victory is mine. How dat song guh again? She said in Jamaican dialect.

**The Prophets**: Victory, is mine, victory is mine, victory today is mine, we told the dragon get thee behind, victory today is mine.

**The Dragon Slayer**: victory today is mine says the King. Thus says the King, Mazzaziel, I will trample you under my feet. Leave my people alone! As of today no more innocent will be impacted says the King. The battle is  our Lord's just as the planet  our Lords and the fullness thereof. This is what the Lord has ordained.

**The Seer**: I have been blindfolded.

**The Dragon Slayer**: the enemy is threatening you and you are responding. Eyes be opened. You are to see that's your job! Do not accept anything the enemy says. Look and see! Every scale get off now! Shards of glass get out!  Nails out, Pepper seeds out! We neutralize the effects of all the objects that are not of the King we cancel, we neutralize it effect.

**Prophet**: getting darker

**The Dragon Slayer**: we cannot leave until the King gives us permission. Now listen when one part of your gift is down you must depend on the others to help you function. You need to depend on the discernment gift to help you if your sight is impacted.

**The Seer:** something I going around my throat

**The Dragon Slayer**: nothing is going around your throat. Loose him, loose him, now, loose him. Spirit of fear loose him now. Oppression loose him.

**The Dragon Slayer** then broke into song singing about the Source caring for the team, his grace being sufficient and he supplies all our needs according to his riches, giving his angels charge over us.

**The Dragon Slayer:** you militia do not be fooled by the dragon. If you want your freedom the Source will give you your freedom and return you to your homeland.

The Source wants to return you to Britain. It will be your choice. Today is the day that you will decide your fate.
 Do you want to continue to work for the King of the 8ᵗʰ Gate and burn in the pit of Hell forever with your master or do you want to return home and get peace while you continue to wander until the Day Of Atonement? Make up your mind. What do you want because today is the day for you to decide?

**The Seer**: he is being held captive

**The Dragon Slayer**: I am hearing that there are three soldiers that need to leave.

**The Advisor**: the other two are walking on the road. They wander the road at night but if the way is made clear for the general who is held here who was their leader who is here they will also go. They will follow his command.

**The Dragon Slayer**: Soldier, today is the day that the King wants to release you. You don't want to go back to Britain.

**Militia**: I don't want to go anywhere. They are exposing you to look like a fool.

**The Dragon Slayer**: who cares. Today the master wanted to release who wanted the release those who work for the enemy who is also being held against their will.

**The Militia** with his beady black eyes said: I will kill you where you stand.

**The Dragon Slayer**: we are not listening to your threats. If you choose to stay with your master here that's fine. It is obvious you want to stay so my Lord, out of their own mouths they confess.

**The Dragon Slayer**: the Lord wants you to return to Britain.

**Militia**: your master is saying pride affected my master.

**The Dragon Slayer**: that is not relevant now. The master wanted to let the slaves go and now I am directed to address you so my master is giving you an opportunity to leave this battlefield unharmed. If you choose not to go then I know whatever happens happen.
One thing I know my Lord gives freewill.
Do you want to go home which is where the heart is or do you want to stay and perish with your friends?


**Militia**: there is no peace as Hell is my bond.

**The Dragon Slayer:** If wandering the earth is your potion isn't it better to wander in a familiar place in Britain than here?

**The Seer**: the slaves that were here were raised approximately thirty years ago.

**The Dragon Slayer:**  Oh. My Lord what is the purpose of all this?

**The Advisor**: Don't worry about what you are not seeing because things are happening and I have stretch forth my hand to heal the land. No matter what the enemy has said I know the plans that I have says the King. That demon was set to trap us today.

**The Seer**: Mazziel is the most stubborn demon ever.

**The Advisor**: A lot of things are going to happen some when we leave, some not how we expect, but a lot of things are going to happen.
I am going to destroy some things because of defilement. I will destroy and rebuild in my own image.

**The Dragon Slayer**: I just heard something and need confirmation what are you hearing? I am hearing now to get off.

**The Armourbearer**: Let us pray.

The Dragon Slayer prayed then said we are being told to sing. Let's, sing oh when the saints go marching in… the team sang in the dark. The Advisor said isn't it fun to worship God.

The Dragon Slayer and friends had an awesome time singing that song

**The Dragon Slayer**: no fear can come here although it is night. We are we are light in the middle of the darkness. She then spoke in an unknown language:

*Darkness and light cannot walk together. You say that light will penetrate the darkness anywhere it is you said a city that is set on a hill cannot be hidden. We are that great city Lord, your kingdom reside within us.*

I am hearing the song shine the light. Shine the light the blessed gospel light.. let it shine from shore to shore.

## Mission Summary

**The Seer**: the advisor is saying that we are to meet the apostle. New level!

**The Advisor**: for you two you are ready for missions, for you my prophetess you now realise your strengths and gifts that you never knew you had and for you if it wasn't for disobedience you would have gone further.

The group laughed.

**The Advisor**: I have to send my people through tests. I must test their obedience to see really if they will go anywhere I send them and if I can trust them.

**The Dragon Slayer**: Thank you Lord that there is no fear because the last time there was a big pink and purple dragon fighting right here above us in the air.

The Advisor is saying it is finished but the enemy is saying it is not. That sound like another battle is coming.

**The Advisor**: what you were supposed to do you did. The angel's role today was just to protect you all today.  The battle is the Lords and he fights his battles in different ways.  You will not always see angels flying around. All that I need to do is send forth the Word. Your physical presence is not always required.

I wanted to speak through the team. That was the King's wishes. Anything that was said today the enemy knows and nothing can reside in a desolate city. I already said from I was giving Ezekiel chapters 6, 4, 3 and Jeremiah that city is desolate because they have defile me and committed idolatry in the city.

They revere and listen to people and rituals than to listen to the Lord of Hosts who they say they worship. However they are going to fall at my feet because at the end of the day every knee shall bow and tongue confess the name of the King.

I have not forsaken the people who need me but we cannot make a few people spoil the whole bunch. Aren't they wondering why the city is desolate and where is the help?

They make me seem like a useless ruler. I only work through people who obey me. I cannot enter anything that defiles, that is why consecration is necessary.

I thank you for coming here today my people. Today was a day of intercession across the nation. My people perish because of ignorance, but you guys heard the calling and the word and came forth to do this in the name of God almighty. You came forth to fight for the King who will not let his people suffer or beg for bread. He sees what you do he is faithful and just and he rewards.

Don't pay any attention to the force or the enemy as I know what I have done and what I am doing. I wanted you guy to know that although the majority of the slaves were gone, some chose to remain and help the enemy in the city.

**THIS STORY IS NOT OVER**. This city as it is shall be no more. This is bringing shame and disgrace to the nation. Just seek me and I will answer I won't leave you out but don't go ahead and do what you feel like not knowing that this I not my desire.

Change your location and continue the debriefing. The enemy will think twice about attacking my people as they have met my Aaron today. Get refreshed. You need to pay the General a visit. There I much work to do.

The team travelled to the General's house. There he awaited the team.  The General went right into action making declarations, providing coverage and warning about the enemy' future plans.

The team was rewarded for their obedience and bravery that day.  Much confidence was received by those who used to be fearful.

The Team celebrated victory that day on the battlefield of the mind and on the physical land. They learnt several lesson from the 8th gate and were to learn more important lessons.

The main lessons learnt from the slave missions include:

*Know your enemy. The King wins all battles.  It is crucial for the children of light to exercise faith, trust and obedience if they want to see victory in their lives. God calls, qualifies, equip and promote his chosen. God is a god of strategy and he makes the impossible possible. He considers history as important and he hates oppression.*

The Dragon Slayer enjoyed the celebration that night with the rest of the team. She knew the next mission would be just an exciting as the previous.  There is more to be revealed about the 8th Gate of Hell and on the little city of Paradise in the Caribbean.

What happened to the African slave that tried to trick the team? Did the principality Mazzaziel leave the city? Is Mazzaziel the same as pharaoh? Who is this Moloch spirit that joined the stronghold and why was oppression the main strategy used to kill, stifle and kill the city of Paradise.

There are many questions to be answered and more to be revealed in the next volume of Dragon Slayer on the leaders and local assignments from the 8th Gate of Hell.  Here you will find out who became a casualty of war. Why did the earth quake? When will this territorial battle end? All this and more in the Dragon Slayer -Warrior for the Lord Volume 3.
Stay tuned.

# Charge to the Reader

*"You are the light of the world. A town built on a hill cannot be hidden. Neither do people light a lamp and put it under a bowl. Instead they put it on its stand, and it gives light to everyone in the house. In the same way, let your light shine before others, that they may see your good deeds and glorify your Father in heaven"*

# Call to Repentance

If you read this book and would like to be a child of God please say out loud the prayer below. Also, feel free to share your experience with us about your decision to accept Jesus Christ as your Lord and Saviour.

# Prayer

*Heavenly Father, thank you for sending your son Jesus Christ to die for my sins. I have learnt today that there is no repentance in the grave and that you are a God of love, so I come to you today asking for forgiveness for all sins I have committed known and unknown.*

*I also release and forgive everyone who has offended me in the past. I now accept you Lord Jesus Christ of Nazareth as my Saviour and invite you to live within me.*

*Please cancel every generational and other curse from my life so I can walk in freedom. Remove any negative spirit and stronghold from my life. Cancel every diabolical plot or assignment sent against me from the enemy and close every open door within my life and cleanse me Jesus. Pour within me your Holy Spirit, your spirit of love and equip me so I can be victorious in all areas of my life in Jesus name amen.*

Now that you have closed all open doors, have decided to avoid past sinful practices and you have received the best gift ever to help you on your spiritual journey, **the gift of the Lord Jesus Christ of Nazareth** let me extend a hearty welcome to the Family Of God.

Please find a bible believing church that can cater to your spiritual development and help you with your walk with Christ. Remember to speak the scriptures (Word of God) and apply them to your situations. Pray, meditate and sing praises to god. Take communion even at home in remembrance of the sacrifice Christ made for you.

*Thanks for reading! Be blessed.*

*Please add a short review online. Like and share our pages as well. Read more book*s written by the author.

*Join our network for the spiritually Gifted and hare your stories with other who will not judge you.*

Log on to:  *www.holitischealingminitries.org*

# About The Author

**Lyssa-Ann Clarke** is a phenomenal woman of God who is called to serve, connect, train & inspire. She is a teacher, author and a Healing and Deliverance Minister who has worked in the fields of Hospitality and Social Services (USA), Banking and Education (Secondary and Tertiary Levels - Jamaica).

Class Valedictorian for the University of Technology Jamaica's class of 2003. Lyssa-Ann is an engaging and enthusiastic speaker, storyteller who shares the Word of God through the use of direct scriptural references as well as in an unusual manner through the gift of Diverse Tongues used to interpret spiritual revelations throughout her messages as she operates within the office of God's Prophet. The "direct prophetic downloads" or revelations from God, given throughout her inspired teachings or ministry sessions, assists the believer in understanding what the Lord requires or advises on a particular topic or situation at a particular point in time.

A teacher by profession, Lyssa-Ann is also a certified Small Business Director and Educator who specializes in Business Administration, Entrepreneurship and Computer Studies. Her experience and certifications include a Masters of Business Administration Degree, a Business Education Undergraduate Degree, Psychosocial Support Training and Evangelism Certification to name a few.

A creative and sociable individual who got her foundational leadership experience as a youth leader in her beautiful island hometown of Salisbury Plain in Jamaica, West Indies; a community that she holds dear and serves.

At the age of twenty-two during a church praise and worship session in her community, Lyssa-Ann had her first encounter with the supernatural where she was told by God that he had a purpose for her.  She subsequently spent years searching for that purpose assuming it had to do with her career and helping others, until the year 2017 when she had a supernatural encounter which saw her verbally affirming her purpose as a spiritual warrior while in a trance speaking to a being of light (God) that emitted a love that no physical man could ever provide.  That year after being instructed by the Holy Spirit to teach the Word, Lyssa-Ann started her quest to push beyond the cultural stigma of teaching about spiritual gifts and spiritual warfare in the conservative or rather traditional church and began teaching topics that the Lord considered important and overlooked yet critical to the survival of the believer.

Her combined research and Holy Spirit led teachings, fuelled the fire for an increased passion for God which led to several supernatural events in 2018 which resulted in her prophetic birthing and an encounter with Jesus on February 6, 2018 where he got a glimpse of Paradise which led to the production of her first book.

A mother to Jayden & J'Ann, Lyssa-Ann also known as Champion from the blog: www.dramaqueenchroniclesblog.wordpress.com aspires to bring hope to many, lead others to discovering their true purpose, provide spiritual healing and deliverance and to inform others of the way to indescribable Love, Life & Truth.

Lyssa-Ann's motto is Luke 4:18 and her mission is to provide healing to the Mind, Body & Spirit through her being used as a channel for the triune God, the Father, the Lord Jesus Christ and the Holy Spirit. She is being led to serve the oppressed, rejected, abused, hurting women, spiritual warriors, unusually gifted  and the spiritually lost.  She welcomes opportunities to participate in your events — retreats, conferences, seminars or ministry and may be contacted at:

**Ministry** : Holistic Healing Ministries

**Website** : **www.holistichealingministry.org**

**Email** : holistichealingja@gmail.com

**Telephone**: 876-845-2696

**Facebook** : Holistic Healing Ministries @salisburyplainjamaica

**Link** : https://www.facebook.com/salisburyplainjamaica/

More Books from the Author available on Amazon:

## Link to Books on  Amazon:

https://www.amazon.com/s?k=Lyssa-ann+clarke&i=stripbooks&ref=nb_sb_noss_2

VISIONEERS
VOLUME 1 - THE GENESIS OF
OBERLIN JAMAICA
Rewriting the Past, Building the Future:
Honouring our Local & International
Abolitionist Heroes
LYSSA-ANN
CLARKE
OBERLIN HIGH SCHO
V I
VISIONEERS
VOLUME II
THE JAMERICAN
CONGREGATIONAL MISSION
EXPERIENCE
Building Jamaica Through Our Heroes
LYSSA-ANN
CLARKE
OBERLIN HIGH SCHO
V II

# More from the Dragon Slayer Series:

www.ingramcontent.com/pod-product-compliance
Lightning Source LLC
Chambersburg PA
CBHW051822150726

47998CB00001B/258